A Consistent Ethic of Life

A Consistent Ethic of Life

NAVIGATING CATHOLIC ENGAGEMENT WITH U.S. POLITICS

Steven P. Millies

Paulist Press
New York / Mahwah, NJ

Cover image and chapter-opening image by Trinity / Depositphotos.com
Cover and book design by Lynn Else

Library of Congress Cataloging-in-Publication Data
Names: Millies, Steven P., author.
Title: A consistent ethic of life: navigating Catholic engagement with U.S. politics / Steven P. Millies.
Description: Paperback. | New York; Mahwah, NJ: Paulist Press, [2024] | Includes bibliographical references. | Summary: "A Consistent Ethic of Life is a guide to help the perplexed Catholic citizen who wonders how to navigate faithfully the complicated ethical dilemmas presented to voters"—Provided by publisher.
Identifiers: LCCN 2023039549 (print) | LCCN 2023039550 (ebook) | ISBN 9780809156894 (paperback) | ISBN 9780809188505 (ebook)
Subjects: LCSH: Catholics—Political activity—United States.
Classification: LCC BX1407.P63 M534 2024 (print) | LCC BX1407.P63 (ebook) | DDC 261.7—dc23/eng/20240213
LC record available at https://lccn.loc.gov/2023039549
LC ebook record available at https://lccn.loc.gov/2023039550

ISBN 978-0-8091-5689-4 (paperback)
ISBN 978-0-8091-8850-5 (e-book)

Published by Paulist Press
997 Macarthur Boulevard
Mahwah, New Jersey 07430
www.paulistpress.com

Printed and bound in the
United States of America

For
Paul Edward Millies
(1948–2023)

Contents

Preface

When I came to Catholic Theological Union five years ago to become the fourth director of The Bernardin Center, the consistent ethic became a permanent preoccupation of my life. It is not as though I had not known about the consistent ethic before I came to CTU, or thought about it at length. As a Roman Catholic I instinctively agreed with the consistent ethic since I first learned about it, and as Cardinal Joseph Bernardin's biographer I had already written about the consistent ethic. But The Bernardin Center has a different sort of connection.

Five weeks before he died, Cardinal Bernardin gave his permission for a Bernardin Center at CTU that would continue his "legacy and ecclesial vision, both of which are rooted in the teachings of the Second Vatican Council."[1] In that letter he also asked particularly for The Bernardin Center to continue to develop the consistent ethic of life. As his life ended, Bernardin knew there was much more work to be done. The Bernardin Center has continued that work, most especially through the generosity of the family of Erica John and Harry John, who established an endowed chair at CTU to promote research into the consistent ethic of life.[2] This book is yet another contribution of The Bernardin Center to our understanding of the consistent ethic, in faithfulness to Cardinal Bernardin's request.

A CONSISTENT ETHIC OF LIFE

The years since Cardinal Bernardin's death have seen several academic engagements with the consistent ethic of life. The ethic has been developed, and this book charts that development. Yet the real feature of the years since Cardinal Bernardin died has been the ongoing, determined effort to distort and discredit the consistent ethic of life, no matter what level of acceptance the consistent ethic has found in the official teaching of the Roman Catholic Church, the very thing Cardinal Bernardin must have feared. As polarization has overwhelmed our politics and our Church over the last three decades, a consistent ethic born in the effort to disentangle Catholic faith from political partisanship has become increasingly difficult for many people to accept. For no better reason than that, this book exists to make the case that we must find a way to escape the limitations of our partisan divisions, and the consistent ethic is the right way to begin. The consistent ethic of life is a fully Catholic engagement with the difficult challenges that conscience encounters in our time. This short book is intended to reintroduce it now, decades since Cardinal Bernardin died, surely an even more challenging moment in Church and U.S. history.

We begin in chapter 1 with the earliest moments when the consistent ethic was born, just two years before the U.S. Supreme Court's decision in *Roe v. Wade* would recast U.S. political life and Catholic engagement with the public square for decades to follow. In those early days, the consistent ethic was a reply to a growing concern that partisan political preferences influenced Catholics more than the gospel. Archbishop Humberto Medeiros of Boston challenged Catholics to be more consistent witnesses to life in 1971, and the need for that challenge would only grow as years went on. For that reason, Cardinal Joseph Bernardin proposed a fuller theological vision of the consistent ethic of life in 1983. In chapter 2 we will examine the earliest development of the consistent ethic as it emerged from the U.S. bishops' pastoral letter on war and peace in the nuclear era, a moment in U.S. Catholic history that again challenged Catholics to be consistent in their witness to life across a range of public issues. Cardinal Bernardin's presentation of the consistent ethic to the nation and the world began a process of refining it that continued until he died in 1996. Bernardin would offer dozens of public remarks and participate in academic conferences intended to develop and improve the consistent ethic of life, a series of events we will review as the consistent ethic developed in chapter 3. Chapter 4 will consider the consistent ethic of life since Cardinal Bernardin's death and will take note of the establishment of the consistent ethic in the official teaching of the Church under Pope St. John Paul II and Pope Benedict XVI. Most important of all, chapter 4 will note some developments under Pope Francis that have refreshed and revitalized the consistent ethic of life.

Yet all those chapters are history. That history is essential. We cannot understand the consistent ethic of life without tracing the line of its theological development from 1971 until today. In chapter 5 we reach the real purpose of this book. As Roman Catholics in the United States look ahead to another presidential election in 2024, and as the U.S. Conference of Catholic Bishops has not fundamentally updated their "Forming Consciences for Faithful Citizenship" document since 2007, this book reflects a hope that Catholics can reengage with the consistent ethic of life in a new way and use it to inform their behavior as voters. "Forming Consciences for Faithful Citizenship" reflects an important ministry of the bishops. The bishops' paralysis regarding that document now for fifteen years (stretching back to before Barack Obama became president and before Francis became pope) is a problem for our Church. That paralysis also reflects problems in our Church.

So let us take our own beginning from this teaching developed so faithfully across five decades and accepted into the official teaching of the Roman Catholic Church by Pope St. John Paul II. Let us ask the vital political questions of 2024 in the forum of our own consciences. Let us commit ourselves to understanding the consistent ethic of life so that we each may become a better witness to life, ourselves.

Acknowledgments

In some ways, this book has been finished for decades. It reflects an engagement with the consistent ethic of life and an approach to politics that I have felt comfortable talking about in class or in speeches for many years. Yet in the most important sense, this book has come together rapidly across the last several months.

I am grateful to Barbara Reid, OP, and Ferdinand Okorie, CMF, the president and the academic dean at Catholic Theological Union in Chicago, who permitted me a "nonsabbatical-sabbatical" during the spring 2023 semester while I rushed these words to the page. The absences they overlooked from my other duties at work made this volume possible. Similarly, I cannot voice adequate thanks for Peter Cunningham, the associate director of The Bernardin Center at CTU, who carried the weight of the Center while I have been writing. This book could not exist without him.

I also have to offer a word of thanks to Father Michael Place, Cardinal Joseph Bernardin's research theologian who helped him develop the consistent ethic. Father Place has become a very good friend in the years since I wrote a biography of Cardinal Bernardin, and his willingness to talk to me enriched this volume in many ways. Meg Hall, the director of the Joseph Cardinal Bernardin Archives and Records Center for the Archdiocese of Chicago, is also a good friend. Meg opened the archives to me once again while I searched for the origins and the development of the consistent ethic in Cardinal Bernardin's papers. She offered some wonderful suggestions, too. I'm grateful as well to Michelle Smith, the archivist for the Archdiocese of Cincinnati, who searched Archbishop Daniel Pilarczyk's papers for records of a consistent ethic conference there in 1988. Rev. Jeffrey Schneibel, CSC, undertook a similar search at the University of Portland. Finally, I am grateful to Dr. Alex Grigorescu and the Department of Political Science at Loyola University Chicago, through whom I had access to Loyola's wonderful library collection during the preparation of this book.

Paul McMahon at Paulist Press was kind and patient, working with me to develop the proposal for this book and then the manuscript. When my father died shortly before this book was due, Paul was generous to offer me additional time. He and Donna Crilly gave me a wonderful experience at Paulist, and I am grateful to them both.

Of course, as always, my deepest gratitude always is reserved for my family. They experience the joys and frustrations of writing with me—and, I don't doubt they would say that the frustrations outnumber the joys. But I could not experience those frustrations or joys without the constant support of my wife, Mary Claire, and our children, Nora and Andrew.

Steven P. Millies
Evergreen Park, Illinois
May 1, 2023
Feast of St. Joseph the Worker

Chapter One

Beginnings
in Boston

The name instantly associated with the consistent ethic of life is that of Cardinal Joseph Bernardin. But the name that should come to mind is Boston's Cardinal Humberto Medeiros. In addition, we could say even more justly that there would be no consistent ethic of life without Father J. Bryan Hehir.

In a sense, it is wrong to fix authorship of the consistent ethic so specifically. We might say that there was a strong ferment underway in the early 1970s giving rise to growing awareness of the parallel between the loss of innocent life in Vietnam and the loss of innocent life to abortion. Certainly this was part of what motivated Eileen Egan in a 1971 interview with Malcolm Muggeridge to say that the various human life issues each represents a thread woven together into a seamless garment.[1] If we really wanted to look for beginnings, it only can be right to start with the Second Vatican Council's Pastoral Constitution on the Church in the Modern World:

> Whatever is opposed to life itself, such as any type
> of murder, genocide, abortion, euthanasia or willful

self-destruction, whatever violates the integrity of the human person, such as mutilation, torments inflicted on body or mind, attempts to coerce the will itself; whatever insults human dignity, such as subhuman living conditions, arbitrary imprisonment, deportation, slavery, prostitution, the selling of women and children; as well as disgraceful working conditions, where men are treated as mere tools for profit, rather than as free and responsible persons; all these things and others of their like are infamies indeed. They poison human society, but they do more harm to those who practice them than those who suffer from the injury. Moreover, they are supreme dishonor to the Creator. (*GS* 27)

Here in one place is the whole perspective of the consistent ethic, a concern that stretches from abortion and slavery to unfit living conditions and the exploitation of human labor for profit. As the teaching of an ecumenical council in communion with the pope, this is the highest teaching authority claimed by the Roman Catholic Church. And as much as this passage affirms the whole consistent ethic, it also underscores its most important characteristic: fundamentally, it is not about any particular threat to life and the person. The consistent ethic is about what does "harm to those who practice" things that "poison human society," those things that "are supreme dishonor to the Creator." The consistent ethic, no matter what the threat may be, really is about our response more than it is about any threat to human life.

The Vietnam War

As much as Eileen Egan can lay claim to the "seamless garment"—many others were thinking in similar ways during the early 1970s—it was then-Archbishop Medeiros who seems to have given us the name *consistent ethic of life*. It is from a homily he preached at a July 4 Mass for Catholic judges, lawyers, and public officials, later published in the Boston archdiocesan newspaper under the title "A Call to a Consistent Ethic of Life and the Law." Medeiros told his listeners that if Catholics "are vocal about the rights of innocent life in the womb yet indifferent to the equally innocent life in warfare, we destroy the consistency of our ethical posture: either all life is always sacred, or no segment of life is ever secure from indiscriminate attack."[2] The larger context of that homily is important.

In 1971 the United States was approaching what could be called the most hopeless period of the war in Vietnam. The United States had been in Vietnam since the 1950s, so 1970 began the third decade of U.S. involvement. The Tet Offensive had long before exploded American confidence about a victory in Vietnam. The peace protests of 1968 had failed to stop the war. Only a month earlier, Americans had begun to read the Pentagon Papers, a secret, internal Defense Department history of U.S. involvement in Vietnam that had been leaked to the public and offered many unsavory, previously hidden details about U.S. actions, including several times American presidents had lied to the public about the war. Ahead were Nixon's reelection, the Christmas bombings of Cambodia, the Watergate scandal, and the slow unraveling of the U.S. presence in Vietnam until an unceremonious withdrawal in April 1975. Medeiros's listeners would have had the Pentagon Papers on their minds, and they also would have known that over 54,000 Americans and millions of Vietnamese had lost their lives in a war Americans had reason to doubt that even their leaders believed could be won.

Opposition to the war in Vietnam among Catholics had been hesitant, to say the least. *The New York Times* wrote in 1966 that American bishops had "largely been silent or, in the case of several leaders such as Cardinal Spellman of New York, supported the war effort," but "the position of the American Catholic hierarchy…contrasts sharply with the peace efforts of Pope Paul."[3] Indeed, Spellman offers the most notable example of support for the war among America's senior Catholic clergy. Spellman had led opposition at the Second Vatican Council to recognizing the legitimacy of conscientious objection for Catholics, and he was reported to have said about the war in Vietnam, "My country, right or wrong. My country."[4] Among the first Catholic bishops in the United States to publish a pastoral letter against the war in Vietnam were the archbishop of Atlanta, his auxiliary Paul Hallinan, and Joseph Bernardin, in which they urged Americans to raise their voices "against the savagery and terror of war."[5] By 1971, four years after Spellman's death, the attitudes of American bishops slowly were changing. The experience of the Second Vatican Council had an effect. In 1971, Brooklyn's stalwart diocesan paper the *Tablet* published a column against the war in Vietnam by Father Phil Berrigan. Still, Robert G. Hoyt was dismissed as editor of the *National Catholic Reporter* only two months before Medeiros's homily for being too "aggressively liberal" on issues like Vietnam.[6] Catholics, who had spent generations facing anti-Catholic prejudice in the United States, had won acceptance as Americans because of their anticommunist bona fides.[7] Catholics in the pews were among the least likely Americans to retreat from their support for the war. They were those to whom Medeiros's words would have been most challenging.

Medeiros's homily was clever for the way it offered that challenge. Catholic opposition to the war in Vietnam was tepid, but Catholic opposition to abortion was not. Aligning opposition to both set a different bar that defied political categories. It set forth a distinctively Catholic perspective on the issues of the day that challenged everyone while being wholly and fully Catholic. The accent of emphasis was not on the war or on the protection of the unborn, but where it truly belonged: on consistency. The either/or formulation was a simplistic binary, but it also captured the essential point: "either all life is always sacred, or no segment of life is ever secure from indiscriminate attack." There was much more to elaborate, of course. But the preferential ethical status of human life in every situation states the consistent ethic of life clearly and forcefully.

There is one additional dimension of context we should mention before we move on. Archbishop Medeiros's homily came eighteen months before the U.S. Supreme Court's *Roe* decision, but Catholics had been active on the abortion issue for quite some time as the issue gained saliency throughout the last 1960s. The state laws against abortion that *Roe* had struck down had been fueled by broad Catholic support, generally by Catholics who identified with the Democratic Party, as Catholics overwhelmingly did throughout most of the twentieth century. In those days, opposition to abortion was seen by those Catholics as being at home with the New Deal and "American liberal values of human rights," defending the humanity of the unborn.[8] Chicago's Cardinal John Cody put the matter as plainly in Senate testimony as Medeiros had in his homily: "Unless America is prepared to protect unborn human lives, it cannot with confidence guarantee protection to any life."[9] To be antiwar or prolabor, to believe in healthcare for all or a living wage for all, to support civil rights and to defend the rights of conscience all was of the same piece in those days. A Catholic voted in a particular way because she or he believed in those things we associate today with the pro-life movement. Consistency was the key.

Father Hehir and Cardinal Bernardin

There is one other key point that needs to be made about Archbishop Medeiros's homily: he did not write it. It should not shock anyone that busy bishops and archbishops do not do all their own writing and, especially when the subject demands specialized knowledge, often the writing is done for them by trusted experts. In 1971 as much as today in Boston, there are few more respected experts on where the Catholic Church meets American politics than the writer of Medeiros's homily, Rev. J. Bryan Hehir.

Father Hehir is a far more important player in the recent history of Catholicism in the United States than his low level of public recognition suggests. A priest of the archdiocese of Boston and active there in parish ministry, Hehir also has advised archbishops of Boston on social and political questions for decades, almost as long he has been a professor at Harvard's John F. Kennedy School of Government. Most important for the story of the development of the consistent ethic, however, we should add that Father Hehir was a staff member at the bishops' conference in Washington during the 1970s. There, in days following the *Roe v. Wade* decision, while the bishops tried to imagine the new way that the Catholic Church would engage American public life, Hehir was both an astute observer and a trusted advisor to the bishops responsible for leading America's Catholics.

In a 1973 homily, Archbishop Joseph Bernardin made the same link that Archbishop Medeiros had made two years earlier between the war in Vietnam and abortion: "The joy that we feel because of the conclusion of the Vietnam war… is severely tempered by the Supreme Court's decision of last Monday which removes the legal restraint to the destruction of life in another way—through abortion."[10] And, in 1975 Bernardin said, "Respect for life has dwindled considerably not only at the two extremes of life's spectrum but also in between....If we are consistent, then, we must be concerned about life from beginning to end."[11] And, quite tellingly, a phrase began to appear in Bernardin's public remarks. In 1976, Bernardin said,

> Life before birth and after birth, from the moment of conception until death, is like a seamless garment. It all hangs together; one part cannot exist without the other. You cannot pick and choose. If we become insensitive to the beginning of life and condone abortion or if we become careless about the end of life and justify euthanasia, we have no reason to believe that there will be much respect for life in between. As a matter of fact, the evidence of history as well as the present moment leads us to the opposite conclusion.[12]

Surely, here we have Joseph Bernardin giving voice to his own convictions about human life. We also see signs that a long collaboration with Archbishop Medeiros's advisor, Bryan Hehir, had begun. We see Hehir's influence in statements like these. Hehir had worked with Bernardin at the bishops' conference when Bernardin was general secretary until 1972 and would work with him again when he became president of the conference in 1974.

A theological ethicist by training, Hehir's dissertation at Harvard University was "The Ethics of Intervention." Intervention in this sense referred to one country injecting itself in an armed conflict on behalf of another much as the US. had intervened to support South Vietnam in the ongoing conflict of the 1960s and 1970s. The ethics of intervention in the light of the Catholic Church's teaching on justice in warfare is the issue that has preoccupied Father Hehir most throughout his published life. The Cold War during which Hehir (who was born in 1940) came to maturity raised new sorts of ethical questions about warfare. One of those questions would preoccupy Hehir and Bernardin in the 1980s: the nuclear arms race. But throughout the 1970s, the ethics of the United States' involvement in a war between South Vietnam and North Vietnam also raised new sorts of questions.

The most generous way to describe U.S. intervention in Vietnam was in terms of a just war. John F. Kennedy, the Roman Catholic president of the United States, wrote in 1961 to Ngo Dinh Diem, the Roman Catholic president of the Republic of South Vietnam, that "the United States, like the Republic of Vietnam, remains devoted to the cause of peace and our primary purpose is to help your people maintain their independence."[13] That language—"devoted to the cause of peace"—is as old as St. Augustine, who wrote in the fifth century, "We go to war that we may have peace," when he instituted the Christian understanding of just wars.[14] Bryan Hehir was twenty-one years old when Kennedy wrote those words, and the reality of the long war in Vietnam that would be masked by such a generous assessment of it as a just war still laid ahead. Hehir would write later in his life about how "the Vietnam conflict forced the just war ethic onto unexplored terrain."[15] We can see the formative impact of these circumstances on Hehir's moral imagination and his approach to Christian ethics in those events he experienced. The question of justice and intervention is the one to which Hehir has referred most frequently in his published work, despite his identification with the consistent ethic. But in this way, we can see the consistent ethic of life as part of Hehir's larger concern about describing a way to promote justice in a world where the Catholic perspective is not shared by everyone, where nations not guided by the principles of natural law pursue their own interests.

As we contemplate the origins of the consistent ethic of life, those early connections that Archbishop Medeiros and Archbishop Bernardin made between abortion and the war in Vietnam seem significant. The shifting moral landscape of the late 1960s and the early 1970s had brought not just the questions of justice in warfare but the whole world to unexplored terrain. The 1968 publication of Pope Paul VI's encyclical on artificial contraception, *Humanae Vitae*, also would bring the Church and its public presentation of sexual morality to a new situation. But more than anything else it was the Second Vatican Council that had transformed the landscape. Already we have touched on the new and unique challenge that Vatican II posed to Catholics: to face toward the world and become more integrated with it. The bishops' conference accepted this challenge when it began to organize itself in new ways to lobby and give public witness more effectively under Bishop Bernardin's leadership as general secretary. This was different from how the Church had spent several preceding centuries and, uncomfortably, it forced Catholics to see themselves in a new sort of conversation with non-Catholics.

The Church and the World

We must recall an important feature of history. For many centuries, the Roman Catholic Church has been uncomfortable with the institutions of modern government and constitutional states. Little more than a century ago, Pope Leo XIII had nearly condemned "Americanism" as a heresy in his encyclical letter *Testem Benevolentiae Nostrae* (1899) and Pope Pius IX condemned the separation of Church and state in his *Syllabus of Errors* (1864). From the end of the western Roman Empire in the fifth century, the Church in Rome was the center of western European political and cultural life. Not only did the Church offer an organizing and legal framework for the feudal dukedoms and kingdoms of the Middle Ages, but it also was—as far as Europeans knew—the universal Church. The Great Schism of 1054 divided the world into Eastern Christians and Western Christians but, even so, the authority of the moral claims that Christianity made on the conscience were undisputed everywhere a Western European could look. The presence of Jewish communities in Europe only proves the point: anti-Semitic prejudice was nourished for centuries in Christian Europe because Christianity was thought to be the authoritative and universal expression of faith, just as wars against Muslims and colonization of native peoples could be justified because they were outside the Church. The Reformation arrived in the sixteenth century to shatter confidence in the universality of the Church's claims on social and political supremacy. The reform movements, as much as they were about Scripture and theology, also were co-opted by the political powers of their day and used to assert the independence of rulers from Church influence and control. The beginnings of our modern notions of separation of Church and state and of modern constitutional government were underway. Rome responded with the Council of Trent (1545–1563), which attempted to reassert the centrality of the Church and set "the course Catholicism would follow for the following four centuries."[16]

The sixteenth and seventeenth centuries were a time of bewilderingly rapid political transformation. The Reformation, as it challenged the centrality and universality of Roman authority, was a driver of these changes. The world that we know today, where constitutions and civil laws establish the boundaries for social and political activity, and the absolute authority of the national state under its own laws inside its own boundaries, came to exist in these days. The religious turmoil of the Reformation made a stronger civil state necessary, one that could withstand the pressures that churches can exert. In a way, the Reformation created the national state as we know it. This was important not only for the power of the nation-state, but also for the ways that we restrain its power. Constitutions have become the mechanism with which we define state power. But definitions tell us both what a thing is and what it is not. The period we are discussing was one that established the supremacy of the national state as the only authority inside its borders, but this Reformation period also created the conditions for the protection of individual rights—especially rights of conscience and religious freedom—that became important limits on state power once disagreement about what people believed became widespread.

The Roman Catholic Church has never quite made its peace with these developments. We see evidence of this subtle conflict still at work in the way the Catholic Church bristles at the authority of the civil state, in the U.S. Conference of Catholic Bishops' religious liberty campaign of the last several years. The claims made by the U.S. Catholic bishops to defend religious conscience have not merely defended the right of Catholics to believe that artificial contraception is immoral, but those conscience claims then have been used to thwart a public policy objective of government, the Affordable Care Act, which provided for artificial contraceptives only because of their proven effectiveness in the prevention of diseases (thus, reducing healthcare usage and costs). This is more than the protection of religious conscience. This is a determined effort to shape public policy outcomes in a way acceptable to just one set of religious believers.

The contraceptive example is useful because it offers us an opportunity to mention Jesuit theologian John Courtney Murray, who had considerable influence on both Bryan Hehir and Joseph Bernardin. In 1960, Murray found himself on the cover of *Time* for his popular book, *We Hold These Truths*, whose subtitle—*Catholic Reflections on the American Proposition*—discloses the theme of his lifelong work. Murray wanted to bridge the historic distance, finally, between Catholicism and modern, constitutional regimes like the United States where Catholics could not dictate public policy. At the time he was on *Time*'s cover, however, Murray was a silenced theologian, forbidden by the Church to publish about religious freedom. Murray's story is fascinating, and it has been told well.[17] But his importance for us begins after his silencing was lifted.

In 1965, the Massachusetts legislature began considering a relaxation of the state's legal prohibition of artificial contraceptives. Boston's Cardinal Richard Cushing wrote to Murray to seek the theologian's opinion about whether the archdiocese of Boston should oppose the change. Murray responded that the archdiocese should stay out of it. In a memorandum to Cushing, Murray laid down a rough sketch of how he imagined the Church should approach such problems in this complex world where Catholics cannot dictate public policy outcomes.[18] Murray pointed to the fact that Catholics would stand virtually alone against artificial contraceptives—almost every other faith community and church permitted them. Murray argued that the voice of religion in public affairs is helpful only when believers from many traditions agree.[19] In all other cases, Murray made a distinction between what he called private morality and public morality. Private morality, of course, concerns a person's belief system and own conduct, and of course here the Church is quite free to define moral expectations that a person may feel bound by faith to meet. Public morality is something quite different, and the difference bears on how the longer history of the Church's relationship to the modern world and nation-state have been a source of tension. All of this is closely related to the reasons why a consistent ethic of life emerged.

Murray finally found vindication for his work on Church and state questions and his enforced silence was lifted after New York's Cardinal Francis Spellman brought him to Vatican

II as a theological advisor. Murray became involved in crafting what became the Council's Declaration on Religious Freedom. The Declaration on Religious Freedom addressed the most difficult question raised after the Reformation—whether the Catholic Church can recognize a human right not to believe in Catholicism. With Murray's help, the Council agreed that there is a right to a free religious conscience to believe as one's conscience sees best. But Vatican II did not settle the larger questions about the relationship of the Church to the modern world. Murray made that observation in 1966, remarking, "No formal document on the relations between Church and state issued from Vatican Council II."[20] Most of the work concerning the meeting of private morality and public morality under a state governed by constitutional arrangements protecting religious freedom remained to be done. It still remains.

The consistent ethic of life emerged in the work of Bryan Hehir and Joseph Bernardin as a means to assist ordinary Catholics, who are the people confronted most directly by the implications of what this history means, across a span of difficult issues that includes the morality of war and the question of abortion. When Archbishop Medeiros first mentioned a consistent ethic in his 1971 homily, the coincidence of a war in Vietnam that raised difficult new questions about justice in warfare with the increasing legal acceptance of abortion was very much in his mind. This was also true about Archbishop Bernardin's statements in 1973 and 1975. Influenced very much by the ideas and the pen of Father Bryan Hehir, both Medeiros and Bernardin attempted to offer some principle to guide the confusing and unexplored terrain where ordinary Catholics found themselves as voters and citizens. With the emergence of the constitutional state after the Reformation and the Second Vatican Council of the 1960s, new kinds of questions about the line where private morality ends and public morality begins faced ordinary Catholics called by

Vatican II to engage the world directly as believing citizens. The challenge was intensified because the issues in play were many and complex. Those issues certainly included the war in Vietnam and abortion, but they also included contraception, the nuclear arms race, pornography, poverty, housing, and healthcare. As each Catholic is obligated by her and his baptismal promises to do good and avoid evil when faced by this overwhelming range and depth of problems to solve as a voter, what Hehir, Medeiros, and Bernardin attempted to offer was a principle to guide ordinary Catholics when they make political decisions. They urged Catholics to keep the primacy of care for human life foremost in their minds consistently, no matter what the question. Consistency is the important distinguishing feature of the consistent ethic of life.

Conscience

On the topic of that principle and the importance of consistency, one final set of observations is important. This sets the stage for our survey of the consistent ethic of life as it emerged in the 1980s and beyond, to the point where, today, it is an accepted teaching of Pope John Paul II that has guided the U.S. bishops in their preparation of their voters' guides to assist Catholics. To set the consistent ethic of life in its proper context, we must appreciate what the Church has always said about politics and political life.

There is a danger that accompanies a guiding principle like the consistent ethic of life. That danger is the expectation that the principle functions like a formula or a theorem: if we follow the recipe and apply the principle correctly, there is one correct answer that everyone should reach if they have done the work correctly. This approach works with geometry, with mathematics, and with baking. But it is never true about politics. Politics includes an extra ingredient that those other activities never include: conscience. The Church always has taught that the conscience of each person, finally, has primacy in moral decision-making. Catholics each have an important obligation to inform their consciences, to understand the moral teachings of the Church so they can know how to apply them in particular questions as life brings them to us. Yet in politics, where moral questions rapidly become moral actions with consequences we can foresee and many we do not foresee, a well-formed conscience is the final authority because no one knows what will happen after we act. Since the ancient world and the writings of Aristotle (political ideas that informed St. Thomas Aquinas, whose ideas have shaped so much of the Church we know), we have described this as prudence. The well-formed conscience acts prudently when it weighs how some action will play out and then tries to choose the best outcome. Because no one knows what all the results of any action will be, good people can reach different conclusions in good conscience while pursuing the same morally good objective.

The consistent ethic of life, therefore, functions like a guide for the conscience. The consistent ethic says that the promotion of human life and human welfare that supports a flourishing human life must guide our conscience toward ethical and political decisions that reflect the most prudent choices that are available. The consistent ethic's most important characteristic has nothing to do with any particular decision we make or even with any particular outcome. Rather, the consistent ethic has everything to do with who makes the decision and how that person makes the decision. The consistent ethic is about us—whether we "poison human society" or give "supreme dishonor to the Creator" when we make ethical or political decisions.

Yet using the consistent ethic as our guide does not spare us from unforeseeable consequences of our decisions that harm people. This is another reason we do not want to think of the consistent ethic like a formula we follow to avoid sin. The war in Vietnam offers a good example. Perhaps President Kennedy did believe that his escalations of the war promoted "the cause of peace." It would not have been absurd for him to believe that. Countless examples in world history tell us about the times when force was needed to protect peace, and the Christian just war tradition has affirmed that idea for centuries. Yet even believing that in good conscience in 1961, Kennedy never could have foreseen the My Lai massacre, the expansion of the war to Cambodia, or the deaths of an estimated three million innocent civilians that resulted from U.S. action in Vietnam. If he believed he was promoting "the cause of peace," Kennedy's decision ultimately did not promote the cause of life. Still, his decision might have been consistent with respect for human life because of why he made it with the information he had at the time. That reality reflects the complexity of our moral circumstances, and why we always need to be clear about what the consistent ethic is and is not.

The consistent ethic of life certainly is not and was not intended to be a simple answer to the complex problem of living in the world as a Catholic believer and a moral person. It cannot be boiled down to simplistic propositions like "abortion is murder" or "the death penalty is wrong." Neither does the consistent ethic favor one political party or ideological framework. In fact, as we have seen, the consistent ethic was developed to frustrate those easy categorizations. The consistent ethic does not conform to our expectations any more than the gospel does.

The consistent ethic of life certainly is intended to challenge each one of us in every moment when it is to be applied. Like Catholic moral theology, our application of the ethic must take stock of our goals, our actions, and our circumstances before we apply it. In the complex interplay of all these forces, we are meant to discern with imperfect information and well-formed consciences. We bring our best, most prudent decision-making, and we choose the thing that accompanies the human person in need the best way that we can. Often, two different people will make different choices even as they both are trying to apply the same consistent ethic and to seek the most morally right outcome. That is the nature of social and political decision-making.

In any event, as we have said, the consistent ethic is not meant to achieve a particular outcome or resolve a particular problem. Rather, it is about the process of moral decision-making. The consistent ethic is here to challenge us to notice the wounded, the marginalized, the poor, and the innocent victims. When we do that consistently, we are putting the consistent ethic to use.

Chapter Two

Cardinal Bernardin's Consistent Ethic

Surely the name most associated with the consistent ethic of life is that of Chicago's Cardinal Joseph Bernardin (1928–1996). Bernardin was the son of Italian immigrants, born just after his parents had arrived and settled in Columbia, South Carolina. Bernardin was ordained a priest of the diocese of Charleston in 1952 and exhibited such remarkable administrative skill that he quickly was named to several senior administrative jobs in the diocese. An unusual sequence of events between 1958 and 1964 resulted in the appointment of four different bishops in Charleston. It fell mostly to Father Bernardin to be a source of administrative continuity during this tumultuous period, and his steady hand caught the attention of Bishop Paul Hallinan (1911–1968), who left Charleston in 1962 when he was named the first archbishop of Atlanta. Attending the first session of the Second Vatican Council, Hallinan contracted hepatitis and his ability to govern in Atlanta was severely limited by his illness. He petitioned Rome for an auxiliary bishop, calling Joseph Bernardin from South Carolina in 1966 to become auxiliary bishop of Atlanta and the youngest bishop in the United States. His career at the senior level of the Catholic Church was just beginning.[1]

Bernardin became administrator of the Atlanta archdiocese after Hallinan's death and remained there until 1968. One of his last acts in Atlanta was to march in the funeral procession for Martin Luther King Jr. In 1968, Bernardin moved to Washington, DC, to be the general secretary for the National Conference of Catholic Bishops and the United States Catholic Conference—the forerunner of the U.S. Conference of Catholic Bishops. While general secretary, Bishop Bernardin built the organizational structure under which the bishops' conference operates today. In 1972, Pope Paul VI named Bernardin Archbishop of Cincinnati, where he remained until 1982, when Pope John Paul II sent Bernardin to Chicago. Bernardin continued to be a leader of the bishops' conference and the Catholic community in the United States, and in 1983 Pope John Paul II elevated Bernardin to the College of Cardinals.

Over the next thirteen years, Cardinal Bernardin cemented his place as the most prominent Roman Catholic leader in the United States and a close ally of Pope John Paul II. Bernardin was a leader in Catholic-Jewish dialogue, and he signed a pact committing his archdiocese to pursue dialogue with Lutherans. As political disagreements and divisions about liturgy began to find their way into parish life, Bernardin created a Catholic Common Ground Initiative to heal the Catholic Church and promote unity on a common ground of faith. When a Chicago-area parish rose up in anger after learning in 1991 that a priest who had previously sexually abused children had repeated the behavior in their community, Bernardin listened and created a protocol for removing abusive priests from ministry and an independent review board to evaluate cases quickly and recommend action. In

1993, when an allegation of sexual abuse that later proved false was made against Cardinal Bernardin, he reported himself to the independent review board he had created. Later Bernardin was diagnosed and treated for pancreatic cancer, a disease that returned in 1996 and ended his life. What people remember most about Cardinal Bernardin was the way he shared his dying with the world, most notably in his posthumous book *The Gift of Peace*.[2] Among his last public statements, Bernardin said, "A dying person does not have time for the peripheral, the accidental. It is wrong to waste the precious gift of the time given to us, as God's chosen servants, on acrimony and division." His insights into dying were a lesson about living he wanted to share.

Life, itself, is God's great gift. It never should be taken for granted.

Challenge and Consistency

The election of Ronald Reagan to the White House in 1980 began a new moment in the Cold War that intersected with a new moment in the Catholic Church. Much as the consistent ethic of life was born from the circumstances of the war in Vietnam, the threat of nuclear war created the conditions in which the consistent ethic became popularized. Reagan promised a nuclear buildup that reescalated the nuclear arms race, and his anti-Soviet rhetoric began quickly to raise the Cold War's temperature in tandem with the arms buildup. The world's anxieties ramped up, and memories turned back to the Cuban Missile Crisis in 1962. The National Conference of Catholic Bishops, the organization Bernardin had given its organizational shape while he was general secretary, provided a means for Catholic bishops in the United States to rally the Church to action. Just days after the 1980 presidential election, the bishops met and resolved to engage the new questions posed by the nuclear arms race through the ancient lens of the Catholic teaching on just wars. What does the teaching on just wars mean in a nuclear age? St. Augustine and St. Thomas Aquinas never had grappled with anything like that question when they wrote about just wars. The U.S. bishops would.

A committee of bishops was formed to study these questions, and Cardinal Bernardin was named as the committee's chair. No bishop in the United States failed to understand the importance of what they were doing, or how controversial it would be. It was a sign of their respect for Bernardin that they chose him to be the chair, and Bernardin's method of leading what became a two-year process was a foretaste of Pope Francis's call to synodality. Father Bryan Hehir, who staffed the committee for the bishops' conference, recalled that the first year was dominated by "hearings" where the bishops interviewed and listened to "witnesses" that included "biblical scholars, a dozen moralists of differing persuasions, a spectrum of arms control experts, to former secretaries of defense, a physician, two retired military officers, a panel of peace activists, and specialists in non-violent defense and conflict resolution."[3] This transparent and open approach continued through the bishops' deliberations and drafting of the document. Two drafts were released by the bishops to the public for comment and reaction. In fact, even the bishops' comments were published for the world to see and consider.[4] This was an extraordinary process conducted in public with the public and among the bishops, the sort of thing Catholic bishops no longer do, which finds contemporary comparison only in the synodal path that Pope Francis has opened. Father Hehir summarized the process a bit modestly when he said, "The method of dialogue was drawn from the conciliar experience."[5] These bishops, who had been formed by the Second Vatican Council, brought their experience of the council to the work of their conference, with and among the people they served. Yet what these bishops did stepped beyond the Council, where only bishops participated in the discussions, to include the public, the whole Church.

When a final draft finally was prepared, the U.S. Catholic bishops approved the text by a vote of 238–9. The result was a pastoral letter intended to speak for the Catholic bishops together as teachers for Catholics all over the United States, called, "The Challenge of Peace: God's Promise and Our Response." It would be difficult to describe it as anything other than a tremendous success. The result of the process made both Catholic supporters and opponents of the arms buildup feel heard, as though their views shaped the creation of the document. "The Challenge of Peace" became a landmark in the history of Catholicism in the United States. It would be joined three years later by another successful pastoral letter, "Economic Justice for All" in 1986, before the bishops' conference began to lose its ability to act together in this way.[6] Yet despite its success, "The Challenge of Peace" was controversial.

"It is inevitable when you discuss matters of this kind… there is going to be a great deal of feeling," Cardinal Bernardin said.[7] After all, the topic of the pastoral letter concerned not only the most pressing issue of its time, but in no small way concerned the fate of the whole world. No living person in 1983 could fail to have an opinion about the nuclear arms race. Controversy followed the letter's release, regardless of the openness of the process or the near unanimity of the bishops. Such is the nature of things, and Cardinal Bernardin knew that. The controversy in some sense continues today, both over the question of whether the bishops should speak together as they did in the pastoral letter and over the questions in the pastoral letter themselves.

Cardinal Bernardin had said the bishops did not want simply to offer a statement *against* nuclear weapons, but they wanted really to create "a positive theology of peace."[8] In sum, that was what "The Challenge of Peace" succeeds as. The letter begins on that note, insisting that "Catholic teaching always has understood peace in positive terms," not understood only as an absence of war or conflict. Peace itself is something.[9] The bishops quoted Pope John Paul II, who had said on a 1982 visit to the United Kingdom, "Peace is not just the absence of war….Like a cathedral, peace must be constructed patiently and with unshakable faith."

When the committee drafting "The Challenge of Peace" made their report to the bishops at the November 1981 meeting, one year after the committee had been formed and having heard from most of the witnesses, and two years before "The Challenge of Peace" would be published, a rather portentous alignment occurred. It should seem familiar. Prior to hearing Cardinal Bernardin's report about the progress of the pastoral letter on nuclear disarmament, in the words of a *New York Times* report, "The Roman Catholic bishops of the United States closed ranks…and affirmed support for a constitutional amendment…that would authorize Congress and individual states to regulate abortion," and "The action followed two days of lobbying to mollify several bishops who objected…on the ground that it fell too far short of the bishops' goal of a total ban on abortion."[10] The same news report tells how later, the same day that Cardinal Bernardin reported on the pastoral letter, "Bishop Edward W. O'Rourke of Peoria, Ill. warned the bishops against 'being stampeded' toward total condemnation of nuclear arms and willingness to endorse unilateral disarmament."[11] The jarring dissonance created by opposing abortion while embracing nuclear weapons as necessary was not unlike Catholic support for the war in Vietnam existing together with Catholic opposition to abortion that animated Archbishop Medeiros in 1971. Cardinal Bernardin certainly would have noticed.

Cardinal Bernardin had been involved in the abortion controversy practically since the *Roe v. Wade* decision in January 1973. During the first presidential election after *Roe* in 1976, Bernardin was the president of the National Conference of Catholic Bishops and led a delegation of bishops to meet separately with Democratic presidential nominee, Gov. Jimmy Carter, and the Republican nominee, President Gerald Ford. The bishops asked each candidate to endorse their hopes to oppose *Roe* and nullify it with a constitutional amendment. Finding success only with President Ford, the pattern of abortion politics was set by those encounters between bishops and candidates. From that beginning, abortion would animate Catholic voters in the United States and their political energy mostly would benefit Republican candidates and causes across the next several decades.[12]

It is difficult to speculate about motive, and there is no textual or archival evidence that supports a conclusion. But it is difficult to escape the idea that Bernardin must have felt some responsibility, if not guilt, for how his involvement in the 1976 presidential election had unleashed a divisive political conflict in the United States that expressed Catholic faith so inconsistently. This idea is confirmed by a private memorandum that Bryan Hehir wrote to Bernardin on September 5, 1976, between the Carter and Ford meetings. Hehir foresaw clearly how it all would unfold next:

> We are now deeply involved in the most specific level of political choice. The public perception is that we are partisan protagonists not moral teachers. The stress here is on the public *perception*: it *exists* apart from our intentions, plans, or desires.... Partisanship at the moment means we are perceived as being *against* Carter; the next question is whether we will be perceived as being *for* Ford after

this week's meeting. The chances of this happening are, in my view, very high….We could emerge from this week not only as partisans on an issue but as promoters of a party.[13]

The prescience of these sentiments viewed today is startling, and they leave little room for doubt that thoughtful Catholic bishops, and especially Joseph Bernardin, must have felt strongly about the need to reclaim their role as "moral teachers" in the public mind. Proposing a way to approach moral problems in political questions that showed no favor to either party or any partisan perspective would have seemed like a very good way to do that.

The Gannon Lecture

Cardinal Joseph Bernardin proposed a consistent ethic of life to the American public and the world in an invited lecture at New York City's Fordham University on December 6, 1983, about six months after the release of "The Challenge of Peace." As we know, the consistent ethic was already twelve years old when Bernardin spoke at Fordham. But now the consistent ethic of life was not only for the hearers of one homily in Boston or Cincinnati, and now the consistency it envisioned was not only something living in the mind of a scholar like Bryan Hehir. Bernardin offered the Gannon Lecture to a broad public audience at Fordham, and the next morning the consistent ethic was front-page news in the *New York Times*. A public ethic was born.

As we shall see, much more would be said and written about the consistent ethic of life after Bernardin's Gannon Lecture. But the title—"A Consistent Ethic of Life: An American Catholic Dialogue"—as much as its text is worth special attention. In addition to announcing a new articulation of ancient Catholic moral principles, Bernardin had a separate goal—to embark on a dialogue between the Catholic Church and the people of the United States. This is what is meant when we say that the consistent ethic of life is a public ethic. The consistent ethic surely is concerned with public issues, things that concern the whole community and not only Catholics. But this public ethic's purpose is distinctive and important: to present ancient Catholic moral principles as a part of the public debate, for use in the public debate, for the benefit of all peoples. The consistent ethic of life was in 1983 (and is for us today) a way Catholic believers can speak to the world outside the Church about important moral issues, be understood by Catholics and non-Catholics, and so contribute something distinctively Catholic to the public debate. The consistent ethic of life, understood this way, is a strategy for faithful Catholic citizenship. It is a roadmap for every Catholic about how to think about public issues and to present a Catholic way of thinking about issues to non-Catholic fellow citizens in the ongoing dialogue of political conversation in the public square.[14]

The lecture itself represented a natural development from "The Challenge of Peace" for Cardinal Bernardin. Around this time, Bernardin had written elsewhere that "the basic premise of world order in Catholic teaching is a theological truth: the unity of the human family—rooted in common creation, destined for the kingdom, and united by moral bonds of rights and duties. This basic truth about the unity and interdependence of the human family pervades the entire teaching about war and peace."[15] The challenge of peace in the world order cannot be separated from the theological truth that unites all human beings and creates obligations among us. This insight is the genesis of Bernardin's presentation of the consistent ethic in his Gannon Lecture.

The Gannon Lecture began with a promise to "discuss ['The Challenge of Peace']…as a starting point for shaping a consistent ethic of life in our culture."[16] The constant emphasis of the lecture was to continue the most essential work begun in "The Challenge of Peace," to bring the moral voice of the Catholic Church to public problems. This was something the bishops were conscious of doing with "The Challenge of Peace," not only because of the urgency of the nuclear issue, but because it was a responsibility the Second Vatican Council had identified for the Church in the Pastoral Constitution on the Church in the Modern World, *Gaudium et Spes*—to "anchor the dignity of human nature against all tides of opinion" (41) by sharing, as Bernardin put it, "the moral wisdom of the Catholic tradition."[17] The Council had asked Catholics in all states of life to engage the world outside the walls of the sanctuary more directly as much as the Council certainly sought to turn the Church's institutional structures toward a more direct engagement with the world. The consistent ethic of life was Cardinal Bernardin's effort to do both at once, to speak through the Church as a senior leader of the Church in a way intended to help Catholics (and others) sort through the complex moral problems that social and political life poses everyone with today.

Because the Gannon Lecture took its beginnings from "The Challenge of Peace" (as Father Hehir's creation of the consistent ethic in 1971 was due to the circumstances of the war in Vietnam), the Church's long engagement with the problem of violence looms in the background of the consistent ethic of life. The fundamental question of the ethic is one that has been with the Church since it first began to attract believers who belonged to the armies of the Roman Empire: When may a Christian take a life? In the Gannon Lecture, Bernardin begins from that place in a review of the Christian tradition of nonviolence that notes, correctly, how "there should always be a *presumption* against taking human life, but in a limited world marked by the effects of sin there are some narrowly defined *exceptions* where life can be taken."[18] This has been the way that the Christian tradition dealt with that question from the fourth century until our time. "The Challenge of Peace" had noted how the nuclear threat is not like other threats to human life, but in the Gannon Lecture Bernardin went on to note how "in both modern warfare and modern medicine," technological developments compel us to have "a sharper awareness of the fragility of human life."[19] In the changing technological situation of both warfare and medicine, Bernardin begins to build a consistent ethic as a way to develop the older response of the tradition to how Christians should think about human life and violence.

The problem first arose in the first centuries of Christianity. As Roman soldiers joined Christian communities, the question arose naturally about whether the performance of their duties was against their new faith. The scriptural evidence seems clear—"All who take the sword will perish by the sword" (Matt 26:52), "Do not resist an evildoer" (Matt 5:39), and "You shall not murder" (Exod 20:13). Indeed, some of the earliest Church fathers made no allowance for any Christian to use violence. Perhaps most famously, Origen of Alexandria (ca. 185–ca. 253) held that only "enemies of the faith" would require Christians "to bear arms for the commonwealth," and to kill.[20] It would take more than a century and the conversion of the Roman emperor Constantine for Christianity to make its peace with violence (as well as lying and other earthly necessities) in the work of St. Augustine of Hippo (354–430).[21] Augustine argued that "all wars are waged with peace as their aim," so Christians could participate in war if the war observed certain conditions.[22] The Christian doctrine of just wars began this way, and would develop for centuries, especially in the work of St. Thomas Aquinas.[23] The morally ambiguous situations that the doctrine of just wars addressed are not just historical artifacts. They are universal problems for Christians living in the world. "The Challenge of Peace" recognized that the moral calculations surrounding nuclear war were fundamentally different from the moral calculations surrounding conventional warfare. With the Gannon Lecture and the consistent ethic, Cardinal Bernardin began to expand that understanding beyond questions of warfare and into the broader realm of social and bioethical questions that have arisen in recent times.

For that reason, the Gannon Lecture in a sense goes back to the beginning and takes up in a fresh light the question of what can or should disturb the *presumption against* taking a human life in new situations. Bernardin noted how there had been a "perceptible shift of emphasis in the teaching and pastoral practice of the Church" for thirty years preceding the Gannon Lecture. The Church had been noting these new conditions and these new challenges in several ways during and since the Second Vatican Council by engaging how often Catholics encounter believers of other faiths, or the new understandings history and archaeology have given us about Scripture. Going back to the beginnings where the exceptions to the *presumption against* taking a human life first took shape, Bernardin hoped to develop a consistent ethic considering the challenges of his time.

With the Gannon Lecture Cardinal Bernardin proposed a new engagement with an old problem in light of contemporary realities. The engagement was not new only because of the contemporary realities it engaged but also because of how the engagement was offered. With the consistent ethic of life, Bernardin sought to overcome divisions, whether they are partisan divisions or difference of creed and custom between believers of different faiths. As Bernardin said in the

A CONSISTENT ETHIC OF LIFE

Gannon Lecture, "The substance of a Catholic position on a consistent ethic of life is rooted in a religious vision. But the citizenry of the United States is radically pluralistic in moral and religious conviction. So we face the challenge of stating our case, which is shaped in terms of our faith and our religious convictions, in nonreligious terms which others of different faith convictions might find morally persuasive." Bernardin wanted to create a public ethic, a moral perspective the Catholic imagination could contribute to public debate that did not depend on any religious commitment. In this way, he was successful. Even the liberal political philosopher John Rawls was forced to acknowledge the consistent ethic as a public ethic.[24]

Bernardin succeeded, we can say, at overcoming those differences we find in a diverse United States where the freedom to believe brings many different value systems to the public square. The consistent ethic over time would continue to be recognized as a public ethic not just by Catholics, but far beyond the Catholic Church. Yet Bernardin also wanted to find a way to thwart the way public issues get sorted into simple Republican or Democratic, conservative or liberal boxes. The roots of the consistent ethic lie in how troubled Bryan Hehir, Humberto Medeiros, Joseph Bernardin, and many others were that too many Catholics let their political commitments drive how they applied their Catholic faith in public life. Catholics who could support the war and oppose abortion, or support abortion and oppose the nuclear arms race, seemed inconsistent. The consistent ethic sought to overcome that problem, to get Catholics to think about all political issues consistently as Catholics first without thinking about political party or ideological commitments.

In achieving that goal, Bernardin and the consistent ethic were less successful.

A Controversial Ethic

Perhaps the most honest response to the consistent ethic of life and Cardinal Bernardin's Gannon Lecture was offered by Phyllis Schlafly (1924–2016). Schlafly was an activist in the conservative movement who founded the Eagle Forum in 1972 to advance conservative causes. Naturally, abortion was a critical issue for Schlafly, who was Catholic, as well as for the Eagle Forum, in the same way abortion soon would become central for the Republican Party. Yet Schlafly, like many who sympathized with her politically, did not greet Cardinal Bernardin's opposition to abortion in the context of a consistent ethic of life as good news. In the wake of the Gannon Lecture, Schlafly remarked for the *Washington Post* that the consistent ethic might be "very divisive for the pro-life movement."[25] Schlafly agreed with a spokesperson for the National Right to Life Committee that abortion opponents "have sharply different views on such issues as capital punishment, human rights and society's obligation to the poor."[26] She summed up the problem thus: trying to unite voters to defend life consistently across the full range of social and political issues that threaten life would "sabotage the prolife movement," which was united in its opposition to abortion.[27] A consistent ethic would complicate things for partisans.

It is difficult to escape the conclusion that much of the controversy that surrounded the consistent ethic of life since the Gannon Lecture in 1983 has resulted less from the consistent ethic's commitment to human life than from its devotion to human life despite partisan divisions and political commitments. Since its beginnings in the early 1970s, the consistent ethic of life had called attention to the incompatible commitments too many Catholics have because of their loyalty to a political party or to a set of conservative or liberal political ideas. Father Hehir and Cardinal Bernardin developed the consistent ethic of life to call attention to contradictions that arise when the same Catholics who supported the war in Vietnam also oppose abortion or when Catholics who support abortion rights also condemn the nuclear arms race. The consistent ethic asserts quite challengingly that the gospel is not meant to be fit comfortably into the terms of political debates in the United States. The consistent ethic's most urgent call is not a call to defend life in the abstract, but rather a call to defend life consistently. For most people, that proved to be too great a challenge. Indeed, the controversy that would envelop the consistent ethic quickly had a distinctly partisan character, reflecting the power of the partisan grip over the minds of believers it had been intended to disrupt.

The public announcement of the consistent ethic also fell victim to a regrettable coincidence. Less than a year after the Gannon Lecture, New York Governor Mario Cuomo gave a public lecture at the University of Notre Dame he called "Religious Belief and Public Morality: A Catholic Governor's Perspective." Cuomo was among the most prominent Catholics in public life during the 1980s, and speculation that he would seek the White House followed him for years. Yet Cuomo also was pro-choice, and in his Notre Dame remarks he referred to the consistent ethic (he called it the "seamless garment"), naming Cardinal Bernardin, and said, "Approval or rejection of legal restrictions on abortion should not be the exclusive litmus test of Catholic loyalty."[28] That was a point with which Cardinal Bernardin would have agreed, and certainly it was consistent with the ethic Bernardin proposed in the Gannon Lecture. But without retreating from his pro-choice commitments, Cuomo went on to express his hope that the debates about abortion would not frustrate other efforts "heal and affirm the human life that surrounds us" by addressing poverty and other social ills.[29] Cuomo's political critics pounced. The conservative magazine *National Review* called the consistent ethic "Cuomo's Cloak," suggesting the consistent ethic amounted to little more than giving cover to pro-choice Catholic Democrats by equating abortion with other moral issues.[30] In a way, this attack on the consistent ethic assuaged Phyllis Schlafly's worry that the consistent ethic would fracture the pro-life community. Instead, using Cuomo to attack the consistent ethic began to exert pressure that discredited voices like Cardinal Bernardin's, Catholics who opposed abortion but wanted to talk about other issues, too.

Those attacks against the consistent ethic would go on for decades. A few years later, James Hitchcock in the *Human Life Review* named Bernardin and Cuomo together and wrote, "It has been the obvious strategy of those Catholics rendered uncomfortable by [abortion] to bury it amidst a number of other issues."[31] In 2005, conservative columnist Joseph Sobran wrote, "Politicians like New York's Mario Cuomo felt they had been vindicated [by the consistent ethic] in their empty 'personal' opposition to abortion."[32] Three years later, the founder of *First Things* eulogized New York's Cardinal John O'Connor by writing that "Cuomo declaimed on the 'seamless garment,' an image that suggests that abortion is one issue among others, such as opposing handguns, capital punishment, drunken driving, and unkindness to whales."[33] As recently as 2020, John Hirschauer attacked Bernardin and the consistent ethic in the same way, for putting the death penalty and other issues on the same plane with abortion.[34] Cuomo's Notre Dame speech was a gift to partisans who wanted to keep the focus on abortion alone, and to reject the challenging call of the consistent ethic.

But we also should say that the coincidence of Cuomo's speech with the Gannon Lecture probably only hastened the inevitable. Abortion politics already had taken their shape in American life by the time of the Gannon Lecture. Bernardin's proposing a consistent ethic the way he did proves that the problem already existed and needed a solution. Had Cuomo's speech not arrived to make the consistent ethic seem controversial and give its critics something to use, certainly some other justification would have come along. The consistent ethic challenged Catholics to be nonpartisans, and partisans had reasons to work against that challenge.

But there was another problem. We should notice that all those criticisms of the consistent ethic never name it as "the consistent ethic of life." Rather, they tend to refer to Cardinal Bernardin's consistent ethic as the "seamless garment." Remember that Father Bryan Hehir had coined the "consistent ethic of life" in that homily for Cardinal Medeiros, while Eileen Egan had earlier spoken about a "seamless garment." The phrases are meant to evoke the same idea, as Egan's own description of all the issues affecting human life being threads in the same garment affirms. Yet "seamless garment" also tends to blur some of the subtleties that the consistent ethic of life attempts to be clear about and needs to be clear about. Cardinal Bernardin generally preferred to avoid saying "seamless garment," and it is notable that the phrase did not appear in the text of the Gannon Lecture. It was in an unscripted reply to a question after the lecture that Bernardin referred to life as a "seamless garment," and that one impromptu remark linked the phrase to the consistent ethic from that time forward. *The New York Times* reported on the Gannon Lecture, telling readers that Bernardin had said human life "made a 'seamless garment' that deserved the utmost attention of the American Catholic church."[35] The phrase "consistent ethic of life" appeared in the article, but not on the front page. The "seamless garment" caught public attention in a way the "consistent ethic" had not, and the consistent ethic became the seamless garment in the public mind. The job of critics had become easier.

It bears saying again, there is nothing wrong with saying that human life is a seamless garment as far as that image communicates the same idea, that we should have the same concern for human life always. Yet moral questions must involve making careful distinctions. There are moral differences between abortion and the death penalty, just as there are differences of immediacy between poverty and the nuclear arms race. All those things represent threats to human life, but there are differences that need to be noted when we discuss them. An image of seamlessness tends to blur those differences. Bernardin would spend the rest of his life clarifying the consistent ethic to try to regain some of the complexity lost in the pages of the *New York Times* and to overcome the impression he had tried to give cover to Catholic politicians like Mario Cuomo. From the moment Cardinal Bernardin presented it as a public ethic, the consistent ethic was a controversial ethic.

Chapter Three

Developing the Ethic

From the Gannon Lecture in 1983 until his death in 1996, Cardinal Joseph Bernardin gave dozens of additional public lectures and shorter talks to expand and to clarify the consistent ethic of life. Thirty-five of them were compiled in a 2008 volume by Thomas A. Nairn, OFM, who has studied and written about the consistent ethic extensively.[1] Nairn offers a brief and lucid explanation about why all those additional public remarks became necessary:

> The Gannon Lecture might have been the only lecture of the cardinal's dedicated to the consistent ethic of life, were there not present in the audience at Fordham University Kenneth Briggs, a reporter for the *New York Times*. The next day, that newspaper carried a front-page article under the headline "Bernardin Asks Catholics to Fight Both Nuclear Arms and Abortion." In the article, Briggs described the talk as opening "a broad attack on a cluster of issues related to the 'sanctity of life,' among them

nuclear arms, abortion, and capital punishment." Briggs added that, "the Cardinal said the various issues made a 'seamless garment' that deserved the utmost attention of the American Catholic Church." The article occasioned intense reactions. Letters were written by those associated with pro-life issues and those associated with justice issues, many criticizing the consistent ethic of life, but some praising the cardinal's stance. The consistent ethic had captured people's imagination, both positively and negatively.[2]

Certainly Nairn was correct that the consistent ethic had captured both positive and negative imagination. But so often in life, it is the negative that gains greater attention and drives the conversation.

The way in which the consistent ethic was calculated to challenge and to overcome the framework of conservative-liberal, or left-right, or Democratic-Republican drove many objections. The consistent ethic was born in frustration with the inconsistent way the gospel was being applied to social questions, and that frustration certainly was also evident in Cardinal Bernardin's Gannon Lecture: a call for consistency must reflect concern about inconsistency. That inconsistency among Catholics in the United States almost invariably appeared to have been motivated by partisan commitments in the context of social and political divisions. The reception of the consistent ethic of life was complicated immediately by the resistance it faced among Catholics who could not look in new way at their partisan commitments, in the consistent light of the gospel of life.

But there was another problem. The Catholic moral tradition is long and deep. It is filled with complexity: the analyses of questions in their particular details reveal how apparently similar cases can be quite different. In addition, the moral tradition recognizes hierarchies of values: some things are more important than others, and the consistent ethic must take note of those differences. It simply was not possible for one public lecture—no matter how carefully and thoughtfully prepared—to embrace all that complexity or respond to every concern about the consistent ethic of life. It simply would be necessary to say more.

A Consistent Theme

Only three months after giving the Gannon Lecture at Fordham, Bernardin returned to the topic of the consistent ethic of life when he offered the William Wade Lecture at St. Louis University on March 11, 1984. Bernardin was careful to emphasize in this second lecture that neither "the Fordham address nor this one is intended to constrain wise and vigorous efforts to protect and promote life through specific, precise forms of action."[3] It was clear that he had the objections to the Gannon Lecture very much in mind when he agreed that "a consistent ethic of life does not equate the problem of taking life (e.g., through abortion and in war) with the problem of promoting human dignity (through humane programs of nutrition, health care, and housing)," but Bernardin still insisted, "A consistent ethic identifies both the protection of life and its promotion as moral questions. It argues for a continuum of life which must be sustained in the face of diverse and distinct threats."[4] The criticisms especially about the hierarchy of threats had attracted Bernardin's concern, yet he insisted on the consistency that should overcome partisan commitments.

As Bernardin's restatements and clarifications of the consistent ethic continued, in retrospect it becomes clear that part of the ongoing trouble with the consistent ethic was that the criticisms about its overlooking the hierarchy and differences about moral urgency corresponded to the partisan commitments the ethic sought to overcome. Catholics more sympathetic to the right were more concerned about abortion than they were about the death penalty or the arms race. More left-leaning Catholics had an opposite orientation. In the end, the linkage among issues and the consistent attitude about human life that Bernardin sought to cultivate with a consistent ethic itself became a mirror of the divisions in the Church as much as the consistent ethic itself became a Rorschach test for Catholics in the United States.

This trouble that became characteristic of discussions about the consistent ethic became evident in the speaking engagements that Bernardin took to speak about the ethic as much as in the development of the ethic, itself. After the Wade Lecture, Bernardin's next public remarks about the ethic came at the National Right to Life Convention in 1984, where he spoke about "Linkage and the Logic of the Abortion Debate." *Linkage* is a word that dominates much early conversation about the consistent ethic, referring to the way the consistent ethic of life links abortion to other issues like war, poverty, and the death penalty. The objection went something like this: abortion is grave moral evil; it incurs an automatic excommunication because it is the taking of an innocent life. On the other hand, while war, poverty, and the death penalty are bad things, they do not equate to the moral evil presented by abortion. The death penalty, this argument says, does not cause the death of an innocent person. Poverty is a social ill with many causes, something that always has existed. War is always evil, but in some cases it is justified. That argument, made by people who wanted to keep the focus exclusively on abortion, said those other issues simply are on a different, lower level. Abortion, they say, matters more. A contemporary statement made by then Archbishop Bernard Law of Boston captured this way of thinking: "While nuclear holocaust is a future possibility, the holocaust of abortion is a present reality. Indeed, we believe that the enormity of the evil makes abortion the critical issue of the moment."[5]

This was precisely the argument Bernardin began to engage with his June 7, 1984, remarks at the right-to-life convention. The "logic" of linkage that Bernardin described offered an entirely unique perspective, one focused not on the issues at all. Bernardin emphasized that the consistent ethic of life was about *consistency*:

> I submit that we must cast our case in broadly defined terms, in a way which elicits support from others….Casting our perspective broadly does not mean diluting its content. Quite the opposite. It involves a process of demonstrating how our position on abortion is deeply rooted in our religious tradition and, at the same time, is protective of fundamental ideas in our constitutional tradition…. One cannot, with consistency, claim to be truly pro-life if one applies the principle of the sanctity of life to other issues but rejects it in the case of abortion. By the same token, one cannot, with consistency, claim to be truly pro-life if one applies the principle to other issues but holds that the direct killing of innocent non-combatants in warfare [such as in a nuclear war] is morally justified….It is precisely because I am convinced that demonstrating the linkage between abortion and other issues is both morally correct and tactically necessary for the pro-life position that I have been addressing the theme of a consistent ethic of life…[and] the need to cultivate within society an attitude of respect for life on a series of issues.[6]

To be drawn into a comparison of the threats posed to human life was to be drawn into a partisan argument about political choices, the very thing the consistent ethic sought to avoid. Bernardin and the consistent ethic called Catholics to adopt an attitude of respecting life in all cases. When the matter is viewed that way, there are no choices to make. We can oppose war, work against poverty, reject the death penalty, and believe abortion takes a human life without facing a dilemma. The consistent ethic asks us to imagine, once we really begin to value human life as the gospel asks us to value it, whether it even is possible to accept anything contrary to the needs of human life. Cardinal Bernardin was telling us it would not be, and that was the witness that Catholics could bring to the social and political world with the consistent ethic of life. The trouble was not that the consistent ethic was not morally rigorous. The problem was not even partisanship. What really stood in the way was us—the men and women who need to face the full implications of what we believe, and then live them.

Still, it is clear this was not exactly simple. Even once we adopt an attitude that links all the issues together consistently and always values human life as the highest good, we still need to navigate a world in which we must make choices, cast our vote, take a side. As we shall see, the Catholic tradition has an answer to that problem. Each of us is called to judge situations prudently when we make choices, and there are guides to help us do that in the context of a consistent ethic of life.

Bernardin would continue to refine his presentation of the consistent ethic, stressing the importance of linking issues consistently as a way to overcome the temptation to single out one issue while also emphasizing the importance of the consistent ethic as a way to present what Catholics believe to the whole political community as a public ethic. The emphasis on a public ethic took on even greater prominence as the years progressed. We can see that in his description of the ethic for the U.S. Catholic Conference meeting of diocesan social action directors in 1988, when he reminded them how the Second Vatican Council "asserted that the social task of the Church in the modern world is to read the signs of the times and to interpret them in light of the gospel," and the consistent ethic responds to that call by doing "precisely" that.[7] Here in these same remarks, Bernardin also has distinguished a different framework for bringing the ethic to the wider public audience. He suggests seeing three distinct and related challenges addressed by a consistent ethic:

- It is a *technological* challenge that "arises from the unique capacities which contemporary science and its medical applications have produced in our generation. This challenge is most clearly visible at the beginning and the end of life. At both ends of the spectrum—the mystery of conception and the mystery of death—our generation has developed capacities to intervene in the natural order."
- It is a *peace* challenge that asks "how to keep the peace in an age when the instruments of war can threaten the very fabric of human life….In very different settings—in the laboratory and in the life of nations—our generation is called to protect the fragile fabric of human dignity against unprecedented dangers."
- It is a *justice* challenge that "calls us to expand our moral concern beyond the question of protecting life from attack to promoting and enhancing the dignity of human life in society. The justice challenge is how to build a society which provides the necessary material and

> moral support for every human being to realize
> his or her God-given dignity."[8]

The consistent ethic of life responds to all these challenges in interrelated ways, offering a clear and distinctively Catholic contribution to the moral dimension of social and political questions facing all Americans. Such was Bernardin's purpose.

At the end of his life, in remarks at Georgetown University that he consciously intended to be his "closing argument" to the world and the Church, Bernardin emphasized again the importance of the consistent ethic as a public witness to the world outside the Church. The Catholic Church, much as all religious communities, should take seriously the "public role of religion" but also should "reflect continuously" about how that public role is exercised.[9] Bernardin offered a perspective on politics and the consistent ethic, saying that "the basic picture of the social fabric of life is crucial to how one makes a moral judgment on the specific issues," and, intriguingly, he used the word that would become important later for the development of the consistent ethic: "solidarity."[10]

If this consistent message of solidarity was expressed, Bernardin insisted, the consistent ethic could succeed as a public ethic where the voice of Catholicism otherwise had failed to capture the political imagination. Defying the unhelpful division of political opinion between Left and Right that fostered so much inconsistency, Bernardin held for a consistent ethic that "cuts *two* ways, not one: it challenges pro-life groups, and it challenges justice and peace groups."[11] The meaning of a consistent ethic is to say in the Catholic community that our moral tradition calls us beyond the split so evident in the wider society between moral witness to life before birth and after birth.

This was Cardinal Bernardin's consistent theme.

Scholars Engage

For all the media attention that the consistent ethic of life attracted quite literally from the day of its public introduction in the Gannon Lecture, it should not seem surprising that the academic community took notice as well. The history of the Church is strewn with controversies that had political and social implications, and attracted lively debates among theologians, philosophers, and other scholars. The emergence of abortion as a political issue alongside the war in Vietnam and the nuclear arms race was an occasion for scholars to reflect and engage with those issues as much as those circumstances impelled Hehir and Bernardin to create a consistent ethic of life, and it was not long before scholars began to publish about it.[12]

In 1985 Mary Segers wrote for *Feminist Studies*:

One wishes...that the church's appreciation of the complexities of deterrence doctrine [as it was described in "The Challenge of Peace"] was matched by an awareness of the subtleties and complexities of the abortion issue. There is no recognition, for example, that abortion is a *sui generis* situation and that, in those countries that have legalized abortion (such as Japan since 1948), there has not been a demonstrable increase in callous attitudes or behavior toward others (the poor or the aged and infirm). The bishops simply assume, with little or any empirical evidence to support their premise, that decisions for abortion desensitize those involved and that the increase in abortions since 1973 translates into callousness toward other lives.[13]

In this way, Segers raised interesting questions about whether the consistent ethic was consistent, itself, in its analysis of the moral problems it engages. Brenda D. Hofman joined the conversation in 1986 with an article for the *Journal of Church and State* that in a similar way argued that by "placing abortion in the context of the 'life issues' as evidence of a consistent theology, rather than in the context of the 'sex issues,' alongside divorce, homosexuality, and contraception, the Catholic Church has been able to justify its abortion position, and hence, its activism, as having a strong bearing on public policy."[14]

Both Segers and Hofman wrote unsympathetically from outside a Catholic (or, at least, Catholic theological) perspective and raised questions that challenged the consistent ethic and Cardinal Bernardin's claims that the ethic spoke to a general public on the public's own terms. More sympathetic was William V. D'Antonio, who reflected on the consistent ethic in an article for the *Journal of Marriage and Family* and found encouragement that "Bernardin's proposal may…provide a new basis for self-identity with the formal church organization," a "basis for a new consensus" among Catholics that overcomes the standard conservative/liberal division.[15] This hopeful assessment from within a Catholic frame stands in contrast with another Catholic perspective offered by Heinz R. Kuehn, who lamented the trajectory of Catholicism in the United States since his emigration from Germany after World War II. Catholics, he said, had gone from "distinction and identity" in the 1950s to little more than "special ecclesial interests" by the 1980s, and showed little interest in "the 'seamless garment' that the archbishop of Chicago, Joseph Cardinal Bernardin" had proposed.[16] What Kuehn called the "'real Church,' the Church of the seamless garment, the Church that has mystery and style, scholarship, and great literature" had given way to something more divided and more vulgar.[17]

These four early examples of how the consistent ethic was received by scholars—two from outside a specifically Catholic perspective and two from within one—in fact illustrate the overall reception of the consistent ethic of life in the academic community and in the larger public square. Catholics received the consistent ethic with a certain amount of hopefulness and skepticism, reflecting the divisions emerging in the Church: Kuehn lamented the "'new church' and the 'new theology' [that] seemed to play into the hands of a world gone berserk with emotions," while D'Antonio (who foresaw "an emerging polarization...[reflecting] the struggle going on in the larger society") at least hoped a new consensus might be made possible by the consistent ethic.[18] Writers like Segers and Hofman, who had no particular commitment to Catholicism in their writing, identified problems and demonstrated the distance a consistent ethic would need to travel in order to influence the wider social and political conversation as Bernardin hoped that it would.

Those academic studies are important for us to note, but they treated Cardinal Bernardin's proposals in the light of concerns more central to those authors. The consistent ethic was not the focus. More deserving of our attention were a series of academic conferences and symposia focused directly on the consistent ethic of life. There have been at least four of them, the first of which took place at the University of Portland in Oregon in October 1986. Bernardin was joined by others like Father Bryan Hehir, Professor Sidney Callahan, and United States Senator Mark Hatfield. The conference affirmed that "underlying serious issues such as the nuclear arms race, abortion, capital punishment, war and poverty is the belief in the dignity of human life, and that dignity must be considered in acting on any of those issues."[19] The new voices who joined Bernardin and Hehir perhaps deserve the most attention. Sydney Callahan, a psychologist from Mercy College, spoke on "A Feminist Pro-Life Position," and argued, "Pitting women against their own offspring is not only morally offensive but philosophically and psychologically destructive."[20] Mark Hatfield, a Republican member of the Senate, spoke against abortion as "violent killing" but also lamented the growing support for capital punishment as "a symptom of a new mean spirit sweeping across America."[21] But we also would want to note that a group called Oregon Catholics for Orthodoxy protested that "the consistent ethic did not include a stand against birth control," prompting Bernardin to reply that "contraception is a different moral problem from" abortion, and "you have to keep in mind the distinctions."[22]

There are no extant records from that conference beyond a news report in the *Oregonian*, and in that way the University of Portland conference is like another conference on the consistent ethic that took place in June 1988 at Walsh College in Canton, Ohio.[23] Cardinal Bernardin again spoke at that Walsh conference, where he was joined again by Prof. Callahan as well as Franciscan Richard Rohr. The Ohio conference had a somewhat different goal, to challenge the Catholic bishops of Ohio "to better understand the consistent ethic of life as a foundation or framework from which to 'teach the inner consistency of all the many respect life issues in our times.'"[24] The conferences offered twenty-six panels and workshops for attendees covering topics that included "respect for life, political responsibility, moral and ethical issues, women's issues, minority concerns, abortion, peace, poverty, and capital punishment," but the substance of those panels also is lost.[25]

We have a very good record of the first truly substantive academic engagement with the consistent ethic at a symposium hosted by Chicago's Loyola University in November

1987. The papers written for that symposium were gathered and published by Sheed & Ward under the title *Consistent Ethic of Life*, edited by Thomas G. Fuechtmann. Those papers explored the consistent ethic critically, and offered an uncommon sort of spectacle in the Roman Catholic Church. A cardinal had proposed a new theological framework, the consistent ethic of life. On November 7, 1987, at Loyola, lay theologians subjected that framework to criticism and the cardinal, Bernardin, sat for a day and listened. This was an extraordinary gift of time given by a busy metropolitan archbishop, and it was (we may say) an extraordinary gesture to listen while reputable scholars like Oxford University's John Finnis suggested that the consistent ethic "misstated" the relevant issues.[26] That conference at Loyola illustrated not simply Bernardin's earnestness about testing the ethic in order to improve it, but also illustrated that important voices in the academic community took the consistent ethic seriously even as they found ways in which its further development was necessary.

Finnis's perspective particularly stands out among the conference contributions, perhaps because Finnis represents the first philosopher to engage the consistent ethic in print, and his skepticism about the ethic revealed important opportunities to improve it. The conference itself summoned an interdisciplinary panel—Finnis, a philosopher; Richard A. McCormick, SJ, a theological ethicist; and James M. Gustafson, another theological ethicist writing from a Protestant perspective. Yet like any academic gathering, the most important questions were the critical ones. The search for truth is not about congratulating ourselves what we got right, but identifying what is wrong. Finnis leveled hard-hitting criticisms in the manner that a philosopher would: he made distinctions. Finnis identified three different consistent ethics proposed by Cardinal Bernardin:

1. Individual Catholics must seek a self-consistent and positive acceptance of the whole framework of linked value, principles, rules, and applications in Catholic teaching over the whole spectrum of linked human life issues, old and new.
2. Catholics have a responsibility to foster in themselves, and thereby in their fellow citizens, an ethos of respect for human life in all its forms and stages, and a readiness to promote the dignity and quality of life of every person across the whole spectrum of threats to life, dignity, and quality of life.
3. To foster the desired consensus among Catholics and thus the desired ethos in society at large, Catholic bishops should publicly commend not only the principles of Catholic teaching on the whole spectrum of "life" and "quality of life" issues, but also policies that appropriately apply those principles right across the spectrum.[27]

Those are, indeed, separable concepts that should be distinguished—the consistent ethic as something individual Catholics pursue as a matter of faith, the consistent ethic as a social value that Catholics should promote, and the consistent ethic as something Catholic bishops pursue in their public actions.

Yet even as he drew these helpful distinctions, Finnis himself ran aground when he encountered what would become a familiar problem in the development of the consistent ethic after Cardinal Bernardin died in 1996. Across the decades that followed, the consistent ethic would come to be used in a way that privileged bioethical questions about abortion and deemphasized other questions related to what Finnis called "quality of life," in addition to peace and justice questions. Finnis debated the merits of "litmus test" or "single-issue" voting in his remarks, and did not approve of them. However, he did find that "since the social and legal application of the moral truth about infanticide is quite straightforward," and "abortion is not more obscure an issue of justice than infanticide," while he yet argued that "it is possible for some members of our society to oppose, *rightly*, social programs which other members *rightly* propose and support in fulfillment of an affirmative norm such as, 'Feed the hungry.'"[28] The effect was to offer a picture of the consistent ethic that was rather inconsistent, and the discontinuity traced the line that divides bioethical questions from peace and justice questions. In other words the consistent ethic, for all of Cardinal Bernardin's efforts to the contrary, would not escape the divisions over abortion.

An Ongoing Development

By most reasonable accounts, the polarization that has come to characterize political life in the United States had begun to fix itself in place by the mid-1990s. In 1992, presidential candidate Patrick J. Buchanan had told the Republican National Convention that the United States already was embroiled in "a cultural war, as critical to the kind of nation we will one day be as the Cold War itself."[29] In 1994, Republican majorities won both houses of Congress for the first time since 1952, offering a "Contract with America" that Rep. Newt Gingrich promised would yield no quarter in opposition to the Clinton administration. Bill Clinton and Al Gore had won a narrow election in 1992, weakened by Ross Perot's remarkable third-party candidacy, which earned 19 percent of the popular vote. Clinton and Gore celebrated their election while the crowd in Little Rock danced to Fleetwood Mac's "Don't Stop," which had been the campaign song. For many, Clinton's victory over George H. W. Bush seemed like a generational transition that would sweep the past away. That may have been right. But Barack Obama perhaps understood the event even better when he wrote, "In the back-and-forth between Clinton and Gingrich, and in the elections of 2000 and 2004, I sometimes felt as if I were watching the psychodrama of the Baby Boom generation—a tale rooted in old grudges and revenge plots hatched on a handful of college campuses long ago—played out on the national stage."[30] Our polarization, for these reasons, can be explained at least in part as a phenomenon of generational change that took hold during the 1990s.

Of course, no single, simple explanation can really be correct. There is more to the story, and while we are narrating the history of the consistent ethic of life we must observe how the growth of abortion politics outside and inside the Catholic Church overlays this generational transition during the time when Catholics were receiving the consistent ethic. Abortion politics had been underway since before the *Roe* decision in 1973, and there already had been pointed public confrontations about abortion before the 1990s. In 1976, Gov. Jimmy Carter had disappointed the Catholic bishops when he declined to oppose a plank in the Democratic platform supporting *Roe*. In 1984 both Gov. Mario Cuomo and Rep. Geraldine Ferraro had drawn criticism from bishops and others for being pro-choice. 1987 had brought a bruising Supreme Court confirmation hearing when Ronald Reagan nominated Judge Robert Bork, and he was rejected at least in part because, according to Sen. Ted Kennedy, "Women would be forced into back-alley abortions."[31] The stage had long been set for abortion to become the arena in which those old Baby Boomer-era grudges might be fought out. In his 1992 convention remarks, Buchanan cited an agenda Bill Clinton would "impose on America," which included "abortion on demand, a litmus test for the Supreme Court, homosexual rights, discrimination against religious schools, [and] women in combat."[32] Celebrating his electoral victories in 1994, Newt Gingrich said, "There are profound things that went wrong starting with the Great Society and the counterculture," called Bill Clinton a "very clever tactician whose core system of activity is a combination of counterculture and McGovern," and called the U.S. Surgeon General an "overt anti-Catholic bigot" because she once had criticized "a celibate, male-dominated church" for opposing abortion.[33]

This intersection between the emerging hyperpartisan polarization and the abortion question had consequences for the development of the consistent ethic from the time of Cardinal Bernardin's death in 1996 onward. Those consequences can be seen both in popular and in the academic literature where the consistent ethic was developed. One case offers a good place to begin, not least because it concerned Bernardin's successor. In 2009, Cardinal Francis George, OMI, published a book, *The Difference God Makes: A Catholic Vision of Faith, Communion, and Culture* (Crossroad). A review of the book in *First Things* took some trouble to contrast George with his predecessor, especially concerning the consistent ethic of life, which, the review noted, "was doctrinally orthodox in itself," yet "had the practical effect of allowing some Catholics to treat questions that were clearly matters of opinion—such as which military interventions were just and at what level the minimum wage should be set—as morally and politically equivalent to the question of whether abortion should be legal."[34] Those old misperceptions about the consistent ethic persisted into this period, placing abortion still at the center of concern. Peter Steinfels wrote for the *New York Times* about how the U.S. bishops, in their quadrennial statements before presidential elections, "had always highlighted abortion as a crucial issue for Catholic voters, but they had never isolated it from a broad range of other moral concerns."[35] By

2004, however, that approach would change because "some bishops worried that its broad range of concerns provided a loophole for ignoring the so-called 'nonnegotiables'" like abortion.[36]

If we shift our attention to the academic discourse around the consistent ethic of life during this period, we find that there practically was none from 1997 until the election of Pope Francis in 2013. At least, save for a reflection on the Mennonite struggle to reconcile their peace tradition with their position on abortion, there were none in academic journals.[37] Without Cardinal Bernardin's prompting, the academic community appears to have let the development of the consistent ethic go for a long period of time with just one notable exception.

Over a three-year period in the mid-2000s, ten scholars met annually to take stock of the consistent ethic and evaluate it carefully after the passage of time. After three years of conversations, those scholars published their essays together in *The Consistent Ethic of Life: Assessing Its Reception and Relevance* (Orbis Books, 2008). In her contribution, Regina Wentzel Wolfe sees the consistent ethic as a remedy for the polarization that has consumed the Catholic engagement with political life as much as it has consumed the consistent ethic, asking, "Why…does it seem to be impossible to use a consistent ethic of life effectively in faith formation in today's church?"[38] Wolfe is as optimistic as Cardinal Bernardin was that the consistent ethic could "effect substantive change" if it were implemented comprehensively and intentionally across every sector of the Church, but the challenges remain. James J. Walter's contribution to the 2008 collection of essays perhaps points us toward why.[39] Walter writes, "Cardinal Bernardin has left us with a great challenge," and he suggests that perhaps that challenge is as yet incompletely understood.[40] Perhaps Walter expresses best what the problem is. He tells us that the moral frameworks posed by Christian theology throughout history have been "content-oriented," which is to say that they have engaged particular moral problems or doctrinal issues.[41] The consistent ethic of life, Walter argues, does something different. The consistent ethic offers "a coherent and consistent combination of normative value judgments about the world, God, and self," which is to say that the consistent ethic of life offers a perspective rather than a set of yes-no answers about issues or propositions.[42] In this way, the consistent ethic reflects theological developments of the twentieth century, but it also faces challenges that earlier approaches did not suffer. This approach adopts what Walter calls a "moral stance," or the analogical reasoning that Thomas A. Nairn, OFM, described as "ordered relationships" among issues that resolve our "accustomed" distinction between moral principles and moral attitudes that make it possible to describe questions in terms of their "family resemblance" to one another.[43]

Approaching the questions of human life through the perspective of an "attitude," or a "stance," or by way of analogy as Bernardin did, was both theologically bold for a cardinal during Bernardin's lifetime (something Nairn noted) and challenging for the Catholics who received the consistent ethic.[44] This approach would frustrate the expectations of yes-no answers on particular issues, and in this way it also would frustrate the binary polarization that was taking hold of Catholic thinking in the United States during the years when Bernardin proposed the consistent ethic. But this approach also was in tension with the *framework* of Catholic moral theology. It is important that we should emphasize the tension with the framework, not the *substance*. Nothing in the consistent ethic challenged the claims of moral theology. Rather, the consistent ethic challenged the way that moral theology was presented. We can say, sensing the emerging polarization that exploited people's desires for yes-no answers, Bernardin was searching for a way to re-present moral theology in ways that would not become captive to our sinful divisions so easily. What the authors in that 2008 collection knew, however, was that theology was reaching a place of making such a re-presentation possible. We might say, they knew that theology was catching up with Cardinal Bernardin and the consistent ethic.

Or as M. Therese Lysaught wrote, "Christian practices emerge as the basis for serving the common good."[45] The consistent ethic of life had begun in Cardinal Bernardin's certainty that respect for life is an attitude we bring to our engagements with moral problems. He had resisted creating a checklist of yes-no answers on critical issues. The consistent ethic of life intended to incite a spiritual response to moral problems, a transformation of the Christian person who engaged the difficult questions of our times. Now theology was beginning to recognize that as well.

Chapter Four

Establishing the Ethic

Catholics presume a lot about what the Catholic Church teaches. "Officialness" is a sort of preoccupation in Catholic moral life, especially because the questions are important and because the moral tradition takes complexity seriously. Of course, because the Catholic moral tradition takes complexity seriously, the moral tradition also is complex. What the Church teaches officially sometimes can be a little opaque even to Catholics with the best intentions who take great care to understand the teachings of the Church.

Pope St. John Paul II's teachings about what he called the "Theology of the Body" may offer a useful and instructive example. The Theology of the Body expresses John Paul's understanding of the Church's teachings around sexuality and contraception, offering a sort of unity oriented both toward the philosophical personalism he had written about before his papacy as Karol Wojtyła and the writings of Thomas Aquinas that guide the Church's moral reflections even today, which had also anchored Wojtyła's personalism in Catholic faith. John Paul presented the Theology of the

Body in a series of 129 *Angelus* messages between 1979 and 1984, and the Theology of the Body has become a widely written about and presented expression of Catholic moral teaching. Countless books may be found on the subject, parish missions frequently address it, and the U.S. Conference of Catholic Bishops devote space on their webpage to presenting the Theology of the Body.[1] Yet, for all that, the Theology of the Body is not, itself, an official Church teaching. We should be clear that nothing in the Theology of the Body is *against* the teaching of the Church, certainly. In a moral tradition where distinctions matter, we should note this.

The way something is taught matters a great deal to the Church. The official teaching of the Church—the *magisterium*—takes many forms and its authority is related to how it is presented. The dogmas of the faith are revealed through Scripture. Otherwise, the highest authorities our Church recognizes are the infallible *ex cathedra* statements of a pope or the declarations of a council. Those are quite rare. More common are those times when the pope teaches through an encyclical or when the college of bishops together, through a synod or some other way, offer or reaffirm some teaching together with the pope. Those contributions to the magisterium do not exhaust the official teachings of the Church, yet they underscore that the manner of a teaching's presentation matters. Not even everything a pope says is something that obligates all Catholics. We know this to be true of Pope Francis's homilies and press conference remarks, most of which are off-the-cuff and unprepared. Pope Benedict XVI was careful about this distinction, too, when he published his *Jesus of Nazareth* books in 2007, 2011, and 2012, noting that these books "should not be considered part of the official *Magisterium*."[2] For as much value as there is in Pope Benedict's books and in Pope Francis's homilies, they are not the official teachings of the Church. Neither are *Angelus* messages during weekly Wednesday audiences with the pope and, so, neither is the Theology of the Body a part of the official magisterium.

The consistent ethic of life, we can say, certainly is part of the official magisterium.

John Paul II

Pope St. John Paul II's biographer George Weigel recounts the genesis of John Paul's 1995 encyclical letter *Evangelium Vitae* ("The Gospel of Life") in his book *Witness to Hope*. According to Weigel, "*Evangelium Vitae* actually began at the fourth plenary meeting of the College of Cardinals, held from April 4 to 7, 1991," in a "lecture by Cardinal Joseph Ratzinger," who told the cardinals that a critical turning point had been reached in the moral debates concerning human life.[3] Ratzinger had warned that "it is no longer a question of a purely individual morality, but one of social morality, ever since states and even international organizations became guarantors of abortion and euthanasia, pass laws which authorize them, and provide the wherewithal to put them into practice."[4] Agreeing with Cardinal Ratzinger, the assembled cardinals voted to ask the pope to address the shift in a new encyclical and *Evangelium Vitae* was the result.

Drafted across nearly four years from that April 1991 gathering of cardinals until the publication of the encyclical in March 1995, *Evangelium Vitae* reflected a careful and deliberate act of official papal teaching. Yet, at least to a small extent, the drafting process could be seen out in public during those four years. The phrases most frequently associated with the encyclical are *culture of life* and *culture of death,* and we know already that Ratzinger had been thinking in terms of a *war on life* and a *logic of death* when he addressed the cardinals in 1991: both phrases appeared in the title of his remarks as they were reported in *L'Osservatore Romano*. Later in 1991, it was Boston's Cardinal Bernard Law who used the phrase *culture of death* to condemn Massachusetts governor William Weld, and John Paul used the phrase publicly for the first time during a 1993 address at World Youth Day, urging his audience to defend "the culture of life against the culture of death."[5]

Cardinal Ratzinger described a "good collaboration" that shaped the encyclical in conversations between John Paul, Ratzinger's Congregation for the Doctrine of the Faith, and others.[6] That collaboration gave *Evangelium Vitae* a distinctive shape that offered more than memorable phrases. *Evangelium Vitae* also represented a major step in the development of the moral teaching concerning capital punishment. The *Catechism* John Paul had published a few years earlier held to the traditional teaching that "the Church does not exclude…recourse to the death penalty, when this is the only practicable way to defend the lives of human beings," though "bloodless means" are preferred when possible "because they better correspond to the concrete conditions of the common good and are more in conformity to the dignity of the human person."[7] Yet during the drafting of *Evangelium Vitae*, an internal discussion was underway that reflected Pope John Paul's personal "loathing" for "the state's power of execution."[8] No matter how great John Paul's "personal feelings" about the death penalty, however, he was able to achieve only a partial victory in the text of his encyclical because no consensus existed among doctrinal leaders that brought capital punishment to a level where it could be condemned in the same language as euthanasia and abortion. Yet we know what John Paul's desires were, and we can see those desires reflected in the text of *Evangelium Vitae*. Reemphasizing the preference for "bloodless means" found in the *Catechism*, John Paul went on in his encyclical to say,

> The problem must be viewed in the context of a system of penal justice ever more in line with human dignity and thus, in the end, with God's plan for man and society. The primary purpose of the punishment which society inflicts is "to redress the disorder caused by the offence." Public authority must redress the violation of personal and social rights by imposing on the offender an adequate punishment for the crime, as a condition for the offender to regain the exercise of his or her freedom. In this way authority also fulfils the purpose of defending public order and ensuring people's safety, while at the same time offering the offender an incentive and help to change his or her behavior and be rehabilitated.[9]

We see here John Paul's clear preference for a criminal justice system that rehabilitates offenders and finds alternatives to execution, and the pope names his reason: "They better correspond to the concrete conditions of the common good and are more in conformity to the dignity of the human person."[10]

Pope John Paul's thinking about the death penalty and his desire for the Catholic Church to promote an "unconditionally pro-life" attitude become important when we read farther into *Evangelium Vitae* and find this passage:

> By virtue of our sharing in Christ's royal mission, our support and promotion of human life must be accomplished through the service of charity, which finds expression in personal witness, various forms of volunteer work, social activity and political commitment....In our service of charity, we must be inspired and distinguished by a specific

attitude: we must care for the other as a person for whom God has made us responsible....In helping the hungry, the thirsty, the foreigner, the naked, the sick, the imprisoned-as well as the child in the womb and the old person who is suffering or near death-we have the opportunity to serve Jesus.... Where life is involved, the service of charity must be profoundly consistent. It cannot tolerate bias and discrimination, for human life is sacred and inviolable at every stage and in every situation; it is an indivisible good. We need then to "show care" for all life and for the life of everyone. Indeed, at an even deeper level, we need to go to the very roots of life and love.[11]

Here, speaking in the magisterial, official teaching office of the papacy, Pope St. John Paul II has deployed language we recognize from Cardinal Bernardin's development of the consistent ethic of life ("attitude," "consistent"), and we see John Paul linking this "service of charity" across a range of situations where we find the human person in a vulnerable condition—"helping the hungry, the thirsty, the foreigner, the naked, the sick, the imprisoned—as well as the child in the womb and the old person who is suffering or near death." We can be certain also that John Paul, himself, was personally unmoved by arguments to exclude the death penalty from this profound consistency in the service of life, just as we know that Pope Francis has invoked his magisterial authority to render the death penalty "inadmissible."

With these words, the consistent ethic of life entered the official teaching of the Catholic Church. No one was more surprised than Cardinal Joseph Bernardin. In March 1995 Bernardin had been given an advance draft of a Vatican document that turned out to be *Evangelium Vitae*. Boarding the return flight from his Jerusalem pilgrimage, he handed the document to Father Michael Place, research theologian for the archdiocese of Chicago, who began to read it. He quickly realized what he was reading and woke Bernardin, who had fallen asleep. He told him, "The Pope has confirmed the consistent ethic!"[12] They had no idea the encyclical would mention it.

In years following *Evangelium Vitae*, this recognition of the consistent ethic would have considerable official impact inside the Catholic Church. The bishops of New Zealand, for example, published a pastoral statement about the consistent ethic in 1997 ("*Te kahu o te ora*—A Consistent Ethic of Life"), and in 2023 they published another pastoral statement reaffirming the consistent ethic.[13] The consistent ethic of life guides the United States Conference of Catholic bishops in their preparation of their "Forming Consciences for Faithful Citizenship" documents, whose most recent iteration claims a "consistent moral framework" in four places and names "a consistent ethic of life" as the inspiration that "has been present, and actively advanced" by the U.S. bishops.[14] Yet even with the intervention of Pope John Paul II, the consistent ethic of life has not gained much traction. Despite official acceptance, less official sectors of U.S. Catholicism have continued to resist the ethic. One critic wrote that "the 'consistent ethic' did help buttress the Bernardin Machine's 'in play' approach to the Catholic Church and public policy, which inevitably blunted criticism of such determinedly pro-abortion Catholic politicians as Edward M. Kennedy and Robert F. Drinan."[15] Another critic has said that there is a "parody" of the consistent ethic that "states, for instance, that the death penalty is just as intrinsically immoral as abortion, or that the minimum wage is just as grave a question as euthanasia, etc."[16] Still one more has written, "Yes, Cardinal Bernardin said, Catholics are obliged to oppose killing the unborn—but in order to be 'consistent,' they must also support housing subsidies, universal medicine, and the abolition of capital punishment."[17]

All these objections center on the complexity of the consistent ethic, a complexity that Bernardin also struggled with: "The *differences* among these cases are universally acknowledged; a consistent ethic seeks to highlight the fact that differences do not destroy the elements of a *common moral challenge*."[18] That complexity is a challenge, it has made the consistent ethic difficult to explain to Catholics. Yet Pope John Paul II was not deterred by that complexity and insisted, himself, that we see the common moral challenge posed by threats to "the unborn, children, the sick, the handicapped, the old, the poor and unemployed, the immigrant and refugee."[19]

The consistent ethic of life is the teaching of the Catholic Church. And the effort to develop and establish it has continued.

Solidarity

We can say that the complexity at the heart of the consistent ethic of life has a simple explanation, one that the scholar's symposium published in *The Consistent Ethic of Life: Assessing Its Relevance and Reception* (Orbis, 2008) identified. From its beginning in identifying the inconsistency of supporting the war in Vietnam and opposing abortion, the consistent ethic has sought to cultivate an "attitude" that prefers life and human flourishing in all situations and cases. At the same time, the Catholic moral tradition is based on principles and a hierarchy of moral graveness: the Catholic tradition firmly holds that some bad things are worse than other bad things. Abortion, for example, is more morally serious than theft. In that published symposium, scholars like M. Therese Lysaught and Thomas A. Nairn, OFM, identified the problem and began to sketch out a solution that reconciles an "attitude" with principles. As the consistent ethic of life has continued to develop since that symposium, the solution has gone on to take additional shape.

One noteworthy development came in the spring of 2017 when Cardinal Bernardin's successor as archbishop of Chicago, Cardinal Blase Cupich, offered the inaugural Cardinal Bernardin Common Cause Lecture at the Joan and Bill Hank Center for the Catholic Intellectual Heritage at Loyola University Chicago. Cardinal Cupich's lecture, "Called to Witness," proposed a new theological lens with which to consider the consistent ethic of life. Cupich said, "I am convinced that just as Cardinal Bernardin proposed that an ethic of life be consistently applied to unite all life issues, we need in our day to mine the Church's social teaching on solidarity, as a means of uniting humanity through a reawakening of our interdependence as a human family."[20] The importance of this development requires some explaining.

Cupich refers in that quote to "the Church's social teaching" that gives us an important clue about what is happening here. Modern Catholic social teaching, indeed, embraces seven themes, as the United States Conference of Catholic Bishops enumerates them, and solidarity is one of them.[21] The other principles of modern Catholic social teaching include the life and dignity of the human person; the call to family, community, and participation; rights and responsibilities; option for the poor and the vulnerable; the dignity of work and rights of workers; and care for God's creation. These principles are intended to identify priorities as guides for Catholics as we reflect on our participation in social and political life. The tradition of Catholic social teaching is vast. These principles gather that tradition together and present it in a way that makes Catholic social teaching easier to grasp and understand.

Solidarity is one of the newer contributions to modern Catholic social teaching. Solidarity itself is not new. It reflects the basic understanding of social life that we find in St. Thomas Aquinas ("The common good is the end of each individual member of a community, just as the good of the whole is the end of each part") and the gospel ("I have given them the glory you gave me, so that they may be one, as we are one, I in them and you in me, that they may be brought to perfection as one").[22] However, solidarity as a named principle of Catholic social teaching and even as a word in English usage is relatively new.

The word *solidarity* came into usage during the nineteenth century, though its roots stretch back across centuries to Roman law defining contractual obligations. Roman law defined a "solidary" obligation as a debt held in common by several debtors equally and mutually.[23] In such a solidary obligation, all the debtors are in it together. The *Compendium of the Social Doctrine of the Church* published under Pope Benedict XVI takes up this notion when it describes Catholic social teaching as a "solidary humanism," asserting that with the *Compendium* that the Church "intends...to propose to all men and women a humanism that is up to the standards of God's plan of love in history, an integral and solidary humanism capable of creating a new social, economic and political order, founded on the dignity and freedom of every human person, to be brought about in peace, justice and solidarity."[24] These passages leave no doubt that the Church intends for Catholics to think of social life in a deeply communal, interrelated, and interdependent way. The Church teaches that each and all of us are coresponsible for one another—everyone, fully, and all the time. This is a challenging notion.

Cardinal Cupich was alert to how challenging that idea is. Yet he also was alert to the ways in which Pope John Paul II had established solidarity deeply in Catholic thought. In his lecture, Cupich recalled John Paul's encyclical letter, *Sollicitudo Rei Socialis* (1987), in which the Polish pope explored the significance of solidarity for social life. Cupich quotes from *Sollicitudo*: "Solidarity needs to be applied consistently to all our human interactions, John Paul wrote three decades ago, calling us to 'see the other'—whether a person, people or nation…as our 'neighbor,' a 'helper'…a sharer, on par with ourselves, in the banquet of life to which all are equally invited by God."[25] The language of this description should remind us quickly of the consistent ethic and its effort to inspire an attitude rather than its strict conformity to an approach emphasizing particular moral principles. John Paul also speaks of a "moral and social attitude" (38) elsewhere in *Sollicitudo*. But perhaps more important is the way in which Cardinal Cupich, observing these correlations between *Sollicitudo* and the consistent ethic of life, has strengthened the consistent ethic by anchoring it in solidarity, a principle of Catholic social teaching, and by making explicit the connection between how Cardinal Bernardin described social life in the consistent ethic and how John Paul taught about social life during the same period in the 1980s that led to *Evangelium Vitae*'s recognition of the consistent ethic.

Suggesting that we think of the consistent ethic of life as an expression of solidarity does not resolve the tension between the consistent ethic's emphasis on "attitude" and the more particular, principle-oriented approach that is common to the Catholic moral tradition. The same questions raised by that tension still exist: When I am faced with a practical choice (like voting) that asks me to make choices about issues like abortion and poverty, how should I choose? Yet even as that tension remains, now the fact of what the consistent ethic is comes into clearer view. Quite often the conversation about the consistent ethic of life sounds just like this: "Which issue is more important?" Placing the consistent ethic under the umbrella of solidarity, Cardinal Cupich has helped us reorient our understanding of the consistent ethic. Quite often we want to see the consistent ethic in pragmatic terms like a voters' guide, a list of issues with a clear set of answers about what we are supposed to do. Yet that is wrong. Perhaps that is the very reason the consistent ethic resists becoming captured by principles and a hierarchy of moral values. The consistent ethic is about something else, and solidarity reminds us of that.

In fact, the consistent ethic is a call to conversion, and Cardinal Cupich drew attention to that when he returned to the consistent ethic in an address at Fordham University that marked the fortieth anniversary of Cardinal Bernardin's Gannon Lecture that introduced the consistent ethic in 1983. Cupich said in 2023 that the consistent ethic "grounds our respect for life both interpersonally and within the human family" by reminding us of "the interconnectedness of all human beings."[26] To think within a consistent ethic of life "is a disposition of gratitude to God for the gifts He bestows upon us, and of service to those who suffer.[27] That is, before we come to issues and moral principles, the consistent ethic first asks us to be committed to our solidarity with one another as Jesus has commanded us in the gospel and as the Church has taught constantly for centuries. And it is a call that corresponds to the entirety of Cardinal Bernardin's ministry, as much as it corresponds to Pope John Paul's teaching. There are reasons to agree that this must be correct. Father Michael Place, a theologian who served Bernardin in Chicago and who was vital to Bernardin's development of the consistent ethic, has said, "I don't think you can take the consistent ethic apart from the rest of the Bernardin corpus…, the passion for reconciliation and peacebuilding. You can't take it away from his personal relationship with Jesus."[28] The "attitude" that Cardinal Bernardin spoke of when he described the consistent ethic amounts to this, our personal relationship with

Jesus. Before we come to the practical questions about what we should do, the consistent ethic asks us to begin in this spiritual way rooted in our own conversion to the gospel.

Cardinal Cupich was clear about what the obstacles are. "We should not be naïve about the resistance that an ethic of solidarity, consistently applied, will meet," he wrote. "It will make demands on how we live our personal lives."[29] John Paul was alert to this as well, writing in *Sollicitudo* that "sin" is the obstacle that causes us to reject solidarity, and "conversion" is the answer.[30] What we are discussing here, and what the consistent ethic proposes, is something more fundamental than how we should vote or our positions on political questions.

We want to be right. This is the logic of our polarized political argument, the very logic in which the consistent ethic was born when Catholics divided along partisan lines to support a war and oppose abortion. Yet the consistent ethic is here to say this is the wrong motivation, even when we make the right choice. And our motivation matters. In fact, in the Catholic moral tradition, our intention matters at least as much as what we do. Really, it is our intention that matters most.

Francis

Cardinal Cupich offered his lecture on the consistent ethic early in the Francis papacy, and certainly before Pope Francis had said much about solidarity. Yet even in those early moments, the direction of Francis's ideas about social and political matters was clear, and Cupich already was able to point toward solidarity as an emerging theme of the Francis papacy. "An ethic of solidarity offers a language and a vision, reminding us who we are as a nation," Cupich said, "but also what it means to live together in this common home, as the Holy Father calls Earth in *Laudato si'*"[31] *Laudato Si'* was Pope

Francis's 2015 encyclical, a document received widely as a teaching about ecology and creation. Of course, *Laudato Si'* does that. But closer inspection reveals something else. Pope Francis was trained as a scientist, he has a scientist's understanding of the natural world, and so this remarkable passage in *Laudato Si'* is worth pausing over:

> It cannot be emphasized enough how everything is interconnected. Time and space are not independent of one another, and not even atoms or subatomic particles can be considered in isolation. Just as the different aspects of the planet—physical, chemical and biological—are interrelated, so too living species are part of a network which we will never fully explore and understand. A good part of our genetic code is shared by many living beings. It follows that the fragmentation of knowledge and the isolation of bits of information can actually become a form of ignorance, unless they are integrated into a broader vision of reality.[32]

Very few teaching documents in the history of Roman Catholicism have discussed subatomic particles. Yet here in this passage, we see clearly what Pope Francis sees: everything is connected. A theme of solidarity begins to emerge, within and with nature.

And of course everything is connected. All of nature as much as all of reality proceeds from the same Creator and the same single creative act. A creation that finds its unity in the Creator who created the universe before time and to whom the universe will return at time's end never really can be disconnected in any time we can live in. In other words, we see in nature a reminder that our social reality also should reflect our interrelationships, our mutual dependency, and our coresponsibility, and Pope Francis tells us so in *Laudato Si'*: "Ecology studies the relationship between living organisms and the environment in which they develop. This necessarily entails reflection and debate about the conditions required for the life and survival of society, and the honesty needed to question certain models of development, production and consumption" (*LS* 138). How we live should reflect the interconnected order of nature.

This was the preoccupation of Pope Francis's next major encyclical letter, *Fratelli Tutti* (2020). As *Laudato Si'* taught Catholics how *everything* is connected, Pope Francis's *Fratelli Tutti*, an encyclical about "social friendship," told Catholics that *everyone* is connected.[33] *Fratelli Tutti* is a powerful case for the centrality of solidarity in Catholic life. The encyclical is a call to a conversion to see ourselves as not merely connected but intimately intertwined with one another, and of course this has implications for all those things that affect human life. Lamenting a "throwaway world," Francis writes, "Some parts of our human family, it appears, can be readily sacrificed for the sake of others considered worthy of a carefree existence. Ultimately, 'persons are no longer seen as a paramount value to be cared for and respected, especially when they are poor and disabled, "not yet useful"—like the unborn, or "no longer needed"—like the elderly.'"[34] He goes on, "War, terrorist attacks, racial or religious persecution, and many other affronts to human dignity are judged differently, depending on how convenient it proves for certain, primarily economic, interests," and, "In the face of such crises that result in the deaths of millions of children—emaciated from poverty and hunger—there is an unacceptable silence on the international level."[35]

Over and over, *Fratelli Tutti* addresses concerns identified with the consistent ethic of life, and throughout it all Pope Francis's message is that solidarity means much more than engaging in sporadic acts of generosity. It means thinking and acting in terms of community. It means that the lives of all are prior to…[the few]….Solidarity finds concrete expression in service, which can take a variety of forms in an effort to care for others. And service in great part means "caring for vulnerability, for the vulnerable members of our families, our society, our people." In offering such service, individuals learn to "set aside their own wishes and desires, their pursuit of power, before the concrete gaze of those who are most vulnerable… Service always looks to their faces, touches their flesh, senses their closeness and even, in some cases, "suffers" that closeness and tries to help them. Service is never ideological, for we do not serve ideas, we serve people.[36]

Solidarity, seen this way, is a call to conversion to place ourselves in the service of the vulnerable, whoever the vulnerable may be and for whatever reason they are vulnerable. This is not a matter of moral principles or hierarchies of values. This is a matter of responsiveness.

The second chapter of *Fratelli Tutti* is an extended reflection on the well-known parable of the Good Samaritan (Luke 10:25–37).[37] The parable illustrates how Pope Francis understands solidarity and how a commitment to solidarity also is a commitment to "an attitude of respect for life across a series of issues."[38] The Samaritan responded to the vulnerable person in front of him, giving aid that was immediate and effective. This is the call of solidarity and the consistent ethic: to be so converted is always to ask, *Where* can *my action* be most *effective* right *now*? It recalls one of the more poignant things Pope Francis has said. In a 2017 interview with

Scarp de' Tenis Pope Francis spoke about giving to the homeless: "You should not simply drop a bill into a cup and walk away. You must stop, look the person in the eyes, and touch his or her hands."[39] This is how we bear witness to life—not because we have correctly chosen the most important abstract issue about which we can be right, but rather by seeking to perform actions that do concrete good for human persons, especially if they cause us some discomfort. This standard should condition our responses to all the issues touched by the consistent ethic—war, poverty, hunger, homelessness, euthanasia, abortion, and all the rest. Our attitude in all those cases is to prefer life and human flourishing, but our action should focus where our solidarity can do the most concrete and immediate good.

From these sorts of reflections the fifth chapter of *Fratelli Tutti* follows naturally, where Pope Francis repeats a call he made first in *Laudato Si'*. That chapter's subject is "A Better Kind of Politics," and to illustrate his point Pope Francis offers us a startling phrase. Francis calls on us to practice "political love," which begins with "recognizing that all people are our brothers and sisters," and aims not at particular individual acts of kindness or charity but rather at the construction of a whole social and political order oriented toward love for each person and the goods that serve human life.[40] In fact, Pope Francis says such political love also must truly be "effective love"—not "mere sentiment" but "a force" that we make effective with our action (*FT* 183). Perhaps the most interesting reflection Pope Francis offers in this chapter and in the whole encyclical comes when he tells us about preferring "fruitfulness" over "results." "What is important is not constantly achieving great results," he tells us, "since this is not always possible" in political life (*FT* 195). Rather, we should prefer a different sort of fruitfulness that can seem strange in our results-oriented political culture. Francis writes, "If I can help at least one person to have a better life, that already justifies the offering of my life" (*FT* 195). This should startle us. Pope Francis literally tells us that the sacrifice of all we have and all we are is worthwhile even if it helps only one person. Yet when we think of the beginnings of Christianity and the sacrifice at the root of our faith, this should seem natural. It depends only on letting go of our preoccupation with results. "We achieve fulfilment when we break down walls and our hearts are filled with faces and names!" Pope Francis tells us. "It is a wonderful thing to be God's faithful people" (*FT* 195). That alone can and must satisfy us.

This is a remarkable way to think about politics. It also is what our faith says. With *Laudato Si'* and *Fratelli Tutti*, emphasizing solidarity the way they do, Pope Francis has effected something like a revolution in Catholic social teaching that can transform how we think about being faithful people in political life. When we reflect on the seven principles of Catholic social teaching—whether we think about the life and dignity of the human person, or the dignity of work and the rights of workers, or care for creation, we suddenly can see that all of them can be thought of as expressions of solidarity. Solidarity becomes the keystone of Catholic social teaching, the principle that animates all the other principles. In this way also—much as Cardinal Cupich anticipated—solidarity brings the consistent ethic of life into focus. The tension between the attitude Cardinal Bernardin spoke about and the rigorous principles of the Catholic moral tradition dissolves, becoming reconciled by the distinction between our attitude and our actions.

Certainly our actions are important. But the attitude of conversion to solidarity that we do or do not bring to action is the measure that matters. After decades of developing and establishing a consistent ethic of life, now Pope Francis has helped us to understand that we become witnesses to life

when we come to social and political questions with our attitude and intentions truly converted in this way. If we understand this well, then we are ready now to ask how to put the
consistent ethic life into practice today, in the face of the challenge we face together now.

Chapter Five

The Ethic in Public Life

What builds a culture of life?

This is the most important question of all. It is a question that matters more than stopping abortions, feeding the hungry, or any of the other actions that the gospel invites us to pursue in social life. This question is more important because achieving a culture of life would mean that the intention behind our pro-life actions is held widely, everywhere. A culture precedes the actions, or else the actions are merely sporadic acts. If we can build a culture of life, all those outcomes will follow.

A culture of life is the goal Pope St. John Paul II named in *Evangelium Vitae*: "We are asked to love and honor the life of every man and woman and to work with perseverance and courage so that our time, marked by all too many signs of death, may at last witness the establishment of a new culture of life, the fruit of the culture of truth and of love" (77). But what would it mean to do this? What really do we mean when we say a "culture of life"?

The Second Vatican Council's Pastoral Constitution on the Church in the Modern World tells us that culture "indicates everything whereby people develop and perfect our many bodily and spiritual qualities."[1] In 1988, John Paul called on "the lay faithful to be present, as signs of courage and intellectual creativity" in human culture, and to bring to that action the "interior freedom" that Christian life cultivates.[2] When we speak of "interior freedom," we might even say that we are describing an "attitude" because interior freedom, in fact, refers to the inner conversion of a Christian. We know that is a proper assumption because John Paul tells us so elsewhere in the same document where he describes our action as being rooted in "an attitude which looks upon the sick person, the bearer of a handicap, or the suffering individual, not simply as an *object* of the Church's love and service, but as an *active and responsible participant in the work of evangelization and salvation*."[3] Everyone is connected. Everyone plays a part. And the distinctive contribution of Christian faith to social life is an attitude that values all life consistently at all times.

Across the last five decades, Catholics in the United States (and elsewhere) have struggled to bring their faith to bear on the complex questions of our time. No small number of voters' guides have been offered to help Catholics do that. Organizations like Priests for Life, Catholic Answers, CatholicVote.org, and *Our Sunday Visitor* have published voters' guides, but of course so have state conferences of Catholic bishops and the U.S. Conference of Catholic Bishops. Even the Holy See contributed something like a guide when then Cardinal Joseph Ratzinger wrote that "a well-formed Christian conscience does not permit one to vote for a political program or an individual law which contradicts the fundamental contents of faith and morals."[4] Inevitably, such guidance offers the same approach to the problem, one oriented toward the moral weight of particular issues. In the following pages, we'll explore why that approach seems inadequate. It does not capture the complexity of voting behavior; neither does it focus on what is most important. Setting priorities in this way inevitably relegates some threats to human life and human flourishing to a lower priority. It becomes possible to treat those other threats as though they don't matter simply because they may pose a less grave threat. This is contrary to cultivating an attitude that values all life at all times.

That is why after four chapters, having come to understand the consistent ethic of life as an attitude rooted in our conversion to solidarity that found support in the official teaching of the Church and was embraced by John Paul II, Benedict XVI, and Francis, we now turn our attention to the practical questions. Now we want to ask, How can the consistent ethic of life help me make choices as a citizen and a voter? The answers will be both simpler and more challenging than what we are accustomed to finding in voters guides. And that should reassure us. Christian faith always should be both easy to understand and challenging to live.

The consistent ethic of life has developed quite a bit across the last five decades. Yet in one sense, it has not changed at all. Just as when Father Hehir wrote for Archbishop Medeiros in 1971, we should be troubled when our support for life is inconsistent. When the converted attitude that can build a culture of life is our priority, consistency will be the result.

Faithful Citizens

Forming consciences is the vital role played by Church and clergy in the politics of our time, and the consistent ethic of life is a useful framework with which to do that.[5] It is a wonderful tool. Once formed, our conscience is something like our attitude. Forming our consciences begins with a spark of awareness that there is a difference between right and wrong, and then it encounters our circumstances and the gospel, which orient our sense of right and wrong toward action. Over time, those actions become habits and our attitude reflects those habits. The Church and our bishops prompt us to form our consciences this way. Yet the last several decades have found the Church and the bishops of the United States taking a different approach, even while the consistent ethic of life has been developed and established.

For as much as Catholics rely on the Church and their bishops to form their consciences, in this complex social and political world today bishops no longer "control the consciences of American Catholics."[6] This distinction between formation and control is important, and it recalls Pope Francis's principle that the Church is called "to form consciences, not to replace them."[7] Women and men today need persuasion more than they respond to directives, even among Catholics. For this reason, a new sort of appeal is needed, and the consistent ethic of life is a response to that need. Yet, since the Second Vatican Council and the *Roe v. Wade* decision, scholars have observed what is plainly obvious— that bishops in the United States have preferred a campaign of lobbying, mobilization, and political pressure to achieve outcomes over a more persuasive, formative approach. Of course such efforts "can only call forth the countermobilization of dissenting Catholics in the opposite direction" and, as the bishops turned to the tactics of lobbying and political pressure, this has been precisely the outcome.[8] This leads in turn to "unintended consequences of having entered the modern public sphere" this way, an orienting of the public witness of the Catholic Church toward achieving a desired result that can come to seem as though it is more important than anything else.[9] The regrettable situation of the Catholic

Church in public life today reflects those "unintended consequences." We need to deal with them.

Most Catholics almost surely do not know the extent to which their Church is engaged in lobbying like "agents of tobacco or gambling interests."[10] Yet despite the relative silence in which the work is done, the Church generally is rather proud of the effort and few other religious groups could "match the Roman Catholic Church in terms of the resources it allocates to political activism."[11] Thirty-two states maintain a Catholic conference—a lobbying organization accountable to their regional bishops—and a National Association of State Catholic Conference Directors functions as a national clearinghouse. Information about the funding of these Catholic conferences is not easy to find, but there is some publicly available information. The Minnesota Catholic Conference reported $730,000 given in 2019 as contributions from the dioceses of Minnesota.[12] In 2017, the California Catholic Conference reported $1,887,000 in contributions from California dioceses.[13] The lobbying funded by parish collections in this way has engaged abortion of course, but state Catholic conferences also worked on a wide range of other issues. Those issues include advocacy for the poor and environmental responsibility, though we must add that recently, state Catholic conferences have been fighting to maintain the statutes of limitation that have prevented sexual abuse survivors from suing for damages. When the Church begins thinking of Catholicism as an interest group the Church begins to behave like an interest group.

Yet more than any issue focus, we should pay attention to the impact of the attitude of lobbying itself. Political scientists and lobbyists tell us that "organizations prefer to lobby for benefits that are private rather than collective."[14] Lobbyists engage in battles to obtain the most favorable outcomes for private, particular interests in the public acts of the federal or state government. Some lobbyists pursue more collective or public-spirited goods, as the Catholic Church often does. But it is the spirit of lobbying we are discussing—what it means to interact and work as a lobbyist with political figures. A narrow focus and an unhealthy competitive spirit can take root easily when the Catholic faith takes on the characteristics of one interest among others in a policy debate. Even when pursuing an interest that is a broad public good, such as advocating for human life, the rough and tumble nature of lobbying can overshadow the best of intentions. When living Catholic faith in public life takes the shape of applying pressure to gain policy outcomes, Catholics risk no longer being witnesses to life or going forth to spread the Gospel. We are jockeying for position, like advocates for any other interest.

The cultivation of a broader attitude of consistency across an entire range of issues can suffer when this sort of approach overtakes our witness to life, and a review of the voters' guides produced by the U.S. bishops confirms this diagnosis. The first of these guides was published on February 12, 1976, with the title "Political Responsibility: Reflections on an Election Year."[15] The document offers a wonderful description of the Church's role in political life, emphasizing the call of Pope Paul VI that "the Christian has the duty to take part in the organization of life and political society" and that every Catholic participates in the "ministry" of the Church to affirm and promote human rights, and denounce and condemn violations of these rights.[16] Then the document comes to "Issues," and the first issue named is "Abortion," where the bishops call for a constitutional amendment to overturn *Roe*. That is not surprising. A range of other issues are mentioned next. They include the economy, education, food policy, and military expenditures, and the treatment of those issues is equal to the treatment of abortion in a way that encourages a consistent ethic of life. In fact that list of issues in the 1976 document follows an alphabetical order and we might say that abortion's first position on the list was only a coincidence.

That alphabetical listing of issues—still with abortion at the top—persisted through the document that preceded the 1996 election. But the document issued for the presidential election of 2000 followed a different plan.[17] The document was fundamentally restructured for the first time since 1976, and was helpfully organized more specifically according to the principles of Catholic social teaching. The list of "Issues" is replaced by a list of "Questions," and here abortion is placed first on a numbered list that suggests priority rather than alphabetical order: "How will we protect the weakest in our midst—innocent, unborn children?" The rest of the list again names a range of issues and concerns that should incite our consistent concern for human life—hunger, healthcare, racism, and so on. But the priority of abortion on a numbered list in this first voters' guide to appear after Cardinal Bernardin's death is hard to miss, especially because abortion appears a second time at the list's conclusion:

> 10. How will our nation resist what Pope John Paul II calls a growing "culture of death"? Why does it seem that our nation is turning to violence to solve some of its most difficult problems—to abortion to deal with difficult pregnancies, to the death penalty to combat crime, to euthanasia and assisted suicide to deal with the burdens of age and illness?

Linking abortion to euthanasia and the death penalty of course is profoundly consistent. Yet, here at the end of this numbered list we find euthanasia and the death penalty in their first appearances, while abortion gets mentioned a second time.

We should pay attention to this narrowing of the focus. And not just narrowing: there is also an implicit prioritizing that became more explicit in the time between the 2000 and 2020 elections. Across those two decades, abortion would become the primary focus of Catholic political life. During that period, several bishops contemplated or imposed ecclesiastical sanctions on Catholics in public life only for their actions concerning abortion.[18] No Catholic supporting the 2003 invasion of Iraq, for example, faced anything like the condemnation faced by Catholics who supported abortion rights no matter how grave an "unjust" war is (the forceful word Pope John Paul used) or how many innocent lives would be lost.[19] In the 2000 document, the bishops write, "We do not seek the formation of a religious voting bloc nor do we wish to instruct persons on how they should vote by endorsing or opposing candidates," and say that "a consistent ethic of life should be the moral framework from which to address all issues." Yet by 2008, the avoidance of forming a voting bloc has disappeared from the text and reference to the consistent ethic itself would vanish. Instead, the consistent ethic still appears but is recontextualized, not treating all issues as "equivalent" but anchoring the "Catholic commitment to defend human life, from conception to natural death" (which seems to be quite broad, yet names two particular issues implicitly—abortion and euthanasia). In the voters' guide preceding the 2020 election, the bishops would write that abortion is "our preeminent priority."[20] This now-explicit prioritization is the clearest separation of the bishops' public witness from the consistent ethic of life yet, as it lifts one issue out of the consistent ethic and elevates it above all the others.

Lobbying and interest group activity are important, constitutionally protected parts of political life in the United States. The question is not whether those activities have their place or can accomplish good things. The question is whether this is how the Catholic Church should approach the world, and what the effects of that engagement are on how the Church addresses Catholics. Naming a preeminent priority at all illustrates considerable distance from cultivating an attitude or even forming consciences. The singular focus on one issue that stands above all other issues indicates thinking as a lobbyist thinks—to achieve a particular policy outcome by mobilizing voters, by applying political pressure, by any means at all.

There is a better way to approach citizenship and voting. That way begins with the consistent ethic of life in its fullness as a part of the Catholic tradition.

Prudential Judgment

At this point in the discussion, the obvious question is one critics have posed throughout the history of the consistent ethic of life: "Doesn't all this just make it easier for Catholics to support abortion?" The answer to that question is a firm no. We will get there in a moment. But first, it is important to deal with why the answer might appear to be yes.

Those who advocate for emphasizing the hierarchy of moral principles when we talk about the consistent ethic of life are correct when they point out that some moral problems are more serious than others. Abortion is as grave a sin as any the Catholic Church recognizes, and the seriousness of abortion's moral gravity must not be overlooked or forgotten. When our perspective has been that of an interest group or a lobbyist, focused on obtaining a particular policy outcome, it is easy to understand how emphasizing an overall stance or an attitude about life rather than a firm principle might look as though we are abandoning something when we set abortion within a group of threats to human life about which we must have consistent concern. Yet this is precisely what the consistent ethic of life does, as it has been accepted as an official teaching of the Church and has sought since Archbishop Medeiros challenged the inconsistency of opposing abortion and supporting the war in Vietnam. We must take pains to cultivate consistency in our attitude, and that does not mean we are abandoning a principle. Rather, we are bringing our experiences to a theological and spiritual reflection. This is what the consistent ethic of life calls us to do as citizens and voters. The question of how to make decisions about voting or where we focus our political action is different.

The Catholic tradition has taught consistently that those sorts of decisions in political life are ruled by prudential judgment. For Aquinas, prudence is "right reason in action."[21] The *Catechism of the Catholic Church* tells us that prudence "disposes practical reason to discern our true good in every circumstance and to choose the right means of achieving it," and this brings us closer to defining prudent judgments.[22] What prudential judgment describes is not simply knowing right from wrong. Rather, prudential judgment engages the more difficult question of which actions are best suited to achieve a good end. We know that our increasingly interrelated modern world is complex. Our political system is made up of checks and balances, our social life gives freedom to people who believe all sorts of things. The action that is best suited to achieve the good end we desire is not always straightforward or clear. Often, reasonable people who agree about the morally right action will disagree about the best means to achieve that action. Some examples may help to illustrate the point.

The Catholic tradition teaches us that we must pursue the best interests of the poor and seek economic justice for all. What is the right way to do that? Many argue that the government is an inefficient distributor of economic justice while lower taxes create an opportunity for investment that will trickle benefits down to the most vulnerable sectors of the economy: as the expression has it, "A rising tide lifts all boats." Many economists agree. They have data and other evidence. But others disagree. They say that low taxes create an occasion for selfishness, that the savings from lowered taxes will be used to buy back stock shares or otherwise maximize the retention of wealth among those who already are wealthy. They also point to data and historical evidence. Which economists are correct? Which path toward economic justice for the vulnerable is the correct one? This is where prudential judgment enters the picture. It is possible to agree about the same moral objective while choosing different paths toward it.

Here's another example. According to the Code of Canon Law (ca. 1398), those who perform or procure an abortion are subject to automatic excommunication, and the principle of moral cooperation has been invoked to link voting behavior to the decision to procure an abortion. When we vote, this argument runs, we assist others to procure abortions and are subject to moral judgment. Our moral goal is reducing the number of abortions to as few as possible if any at all. As a practical matter, what is the most effective way to do that? Some will argue that the incidences of abortion are reduced when candidates who favor generous policies to support families with government assistance are elected. Many years of data show that the numbers of abortions decline when Democrats hold office, especially when Democrats hold both Congress and the White House. At the same time, others claim that the best course of action is to vote for candidates who will work to make abortions entirely illegal. They say abortion is a nonnegotiable moral issue, and no other question matters as much because life is fundamental; protecting innocent, unborn life must have priority. Which choice is correct? Again, this is a matter of prudential judgment. Catholics can agree about the same moral object and disagree in the complex politics of our times about the best way to achieve that object.

The point of these examples is to illustrate how unsuitable an insistence on particular responses to the complex politics of a system of government such as we have in the United States really is. To insist on abortion as the preeminent priority to guide voter behavior without engaging in any of the intricate details of abortion policy, and simply to insist that one issue stands above all other threats to human life in fact does very little to defend human life. Not only does such an approach fail to engage the details of what public policy steps would be effective to accomplish the desired moral objective, but it also fails to consider the reality of what voter choices mean. Very few of us have concrete and immediate opportunities as voters to stop abortion because very few of the votes we cast really could bring about that outcome.

In the eleven presidential elections held from 1976 to 2012, Catholics were told with increasing fervor to vote for candidates who opposed abortions. Yet their votes never accomplished its elimination. Indeed, even in 2016 when Donald Trump was elected and appointed the justices of the Supreme Court who made the majority in *Dobbs v. Jackson*, all that was accomplished was to return abortion to the states: abortions was not stopped, and a culture of life is no nearer to being realized. In congressional races, the connection to abortion has been even more tenuous, confined to the renewal of Hyde Act, the Mexico City Policy, and the confirmations of federal judges. State-level races hardly mattered at all until the *Dobbs* decision. Yet, over nearly fifty years, consider all the other public policy implications of voting at any of these levels.

When we look at the consistent ethic in light of how Pope Francis has taught the Church about solidarity in social life, we come to understand that we need to be more thoughtful about how we orient our actions. We can hold many opinions about how to serve the cause of human life and address all the issues that frustrate or promote its flourishing. Often those opinions will defy easy categorization or sorting into a political party. The unborn do not need us to name preeminent priorities in every election because very few of the elections we vote in affect the number of abortions. Only interest groups need preeminent priorities to make certain that their issue remains at the top of our concern, whether we can be effective about it or not.

Cultivating a consistent attitude about promoting human life and human flourishing is a much better way to approach political questions. Yet, when we approach political questions this way, we accept a greater challenge. When we consistently take our attitude about promoting human life and human flourishing to politics, we accept an obligation to understand the political system and the political circumstances, in addition to the moral tradition and the hierarchy of moral principles. We must stay constantly informed, remain constantly up-to-date, and constantly reflect on the political possibilities of each moment.

Here Pope Francis's encyclical on social friendship and solidarity, *Fratelli Tutti*, is especially helpful. If we remember that encyclical's long reflection on the parable of the Good Samaritan in its second chapter and its call to responsiveness, we find the beginning of how we are intended to be Catholic citizens and to vote. In every situation, we must survey the whole landscape and identify the vulnerable person who is nearest to us, whom our immediate action can help most effectively. If our prudential judgment tells us that our vote can most effectively and immediately help the unborn, then that must guide our voting. If our prudential judgment tells us that the poor or the environment are helped more effectively and immediately by our political choices this time, then that is the right decision.

In the end, we will not be judged by the public policies we changed or did not change. That is not the moral measure. Very few of us as individuals affect public policy anyway. Rather, if God ever asks us about our voting behavior, we have reasons to feel sure the question will be about whether we loved our neighbors *effectively*—whether we pursued our care for the vulnerable in the best way to *actually help* anyone. What will it take to answer yes? We must be shrewd and measure our vote to the possibilities of a particular time and place. In many elections, it has been more possible to help the poor than to stop abortions, or it has been more possible to frustrate an unjust war than to end the death penalty. We must use prudence when we make those calculations with the best information available and with a well-formed conscience. And, undoubtedly, the unfolding of events will sometimes prove us wrong. We must learn from that, and then become better voters next time. So long as we maintain our consistent attitude about the priority of human life and do the work to inform ourselves and form our consciences, remain committed to be in solidarity with everyone, especially the vulnerable, we can feel sure we have performed our moral duty. We have a duty to try to get it right each time we vote. Still, no one knows the future so it is our intention to be effective and our attitude about life that matter more than choosing the most morally important issue to prioritize regardless of whether we can make effective change.

What Priorities?

So how should I vote?

The question seems inevitable, almost natural. It is a consequence of our pragmatic, American way of doing things and of thinking. We want a result. We want a clear answer. Yet, this book about the consistent ethic of life ends now with a firm determination not to answer that question with any preeminent priorities or nonnegotiable moral issues. The desire for a clear roadmap has polluted the thinking of too many Roman Catholics in the United States for too long. Our faith is greater and more complex than a simple answer to a complex question.

The consistent ethic of life began more than fifty years ago as a response to another kind of pollution of our Catholic faith that resulted when Catholics absorbed too much of the partisanship around them. That partisan tinge that infected the witness for life during the Vietnam era once again presented itself during the Reagan-era arms buildup of the early 1980s, and across the decades we only have seen the partisan spirit grow. The problem persists, and we see it in polling. The Pew Research Center found in 2019 that "when it comes to a number of specific issues—including some on which Catholic teachings leave little room for doubt—Catholic partisans often express opinions that are much more in line with the positions of their political parties than with the teachings of their Church."[23] Catholic Democrats are indistinguishable on the issues from other Democrats, while Catholic Republicans are indistinguishable on the issues from other Republicans. The data paint a depressing picture that suggests that in political life, Catholic faith really makes no difference at all.

When we value human life consistently in all situations, Catholics simply cannot look like either Democrats or Republicans. It is fine to vote for Republicans, just as it is fine to vote for Democrats. But when our views align consistently with one party or the other, that is a clear signal that something is wrong. It means that our faith has not penetrated our lives. Our consistent alignment is meant to bring us somewhere else.

The only answer to the question, how should I vote, is to struggle each time in the light of new circumstances and with the possibilities before us in the light of our attitude of respect for life. This is an act of recognizing at once that the stakes are higher and lower than we think they are. The stakes are higher because now, as voters living under modern systems of constitutional government, we are in possession of full responsibility for what we do with our citizenship. The choice rests on each person's shoulders today in a way that political choices never burdened our premodern ancestors. Yet at the same time, it is worth remembering that the stakes also are lower. No one vote and no one election can solve all the problems or address all the challenges facing human life. We sometimes think of politics that way—"the most important election of our lifetime." The truth is that the opportunities we get in politics are always more narrow. Exercising our prudential judgment according to the opportunities and circumstances of a particular moment in the light of our consistent concern for human life is the only formula that there is for a Catholic voter. There really can be no other. This is the only answer to the question "How should I vote?" and the best compass we have available is the consistent ethic, an attitude of respect for life that can lead us in many different directions, disagreeing with one another because we each have made different prudential judgments about the best way to be witnesses to life.

As we look around us at the signs of these times and ask the question, however, some urgent priorities do suggest themselves:

- Abortions continue to be performed around the United States. Some cases reflect difficult medical situations, and we want to distinguish those because the challenges women face in such circumstances are different. Some abortions are genuine choices that women make without any duress at all. But in too many cases, abortion is a sign of helplessness or hopelessness. They are cases that have arisen because of inadequate education, inadequate opportunity, inadequate family support, and inadequate social support. Now that the *Roe* decision has been reversed, there is an opportunity to reexamine the social and economic questions that surround the abortion issue. A great deal of energy has been expended on implementing state-level abortion restrictions, and the U.S. bishops have expressed support for a national ban on abortions after the fifteenth week of a pregnancy (a measure that would permit 95 percent of the abortions permitted under *Roe*).[24] But perhaps there are better ways to join pregnant women across the United States in "radical solidarity" that listens to their needs and their experiences.[25]

- Migrants continue to seek a better life in the United States by crossing the southern border. A range of factors influence their decisions to undertake a difficult and dangerous migration. Yet when they reach the United States, too often migrants are not welcomed. A crisis of family separations persists because of choices the U.S. government made beginning in 2018. Often, migrants are used as political props even by Catholic political leaders. Overall, the United States remains ill-equipped to address the needs of migrants and the needs of U.S. residents because the political will cannot be found to undertake a comprehensive immigration reform.

- The last several years have brought a remarkable increase in antisemitic and Islamophobic hate crimes in the United States. We know that other hatreds and forms of exclusion have not diminished, including racism, gender-based inequality, and the rejection of LGBTQ+ persons. Our divided United States exhibits its divisions in ugly ways that are utterly incompatible with the gospel, with the principle of solidarity, and the simple proposition that free people should live together in peace.

- Wealth inequality in the United States is at its highest level in a century, and it is increasing more rapidly here than other parts of the world. The effects are worse in communities of color. The wealth gap has enormous social consequences that are measured in lives lost to homelessness and poverty. Yet there also are political consequences when we consider the implications of "dark money" in politics and the sort of political influence denied to all but the wealthiest Americans under a system of government that claims equality and democracy as values.

- Climate scientists tell us that the global temperature has risen two degrees since 1880 and the rate of increase is accelerating. The implications already are seen in places like Miami, where flooded streets have become routine due to rising sea levels, but the real implications are found in more vulnerable places around the world. Soon, if predictions hold, the sources of fresh drinking water will be strained in many parts of the globe, a looming crisis with vast geopolitical implications that also will threaten tens of millions of lives.

- Child poverty and infant mortality in the United States are staggeringly high for a nation with such resources and wealth that we have. Especially because of our Catholic concern for unborn children, the scandal of our infant mortality rate (at 5.4 per 1,000 live births in 2020, it is three times greater than Norway) and poverty among U.S. children (at 20.9 percent, our child poverty rate is almost double the global average) should seize the attention of every person, Catholic or not.

These all are worthy issues that should preoccupy us in the light of a consistent ethic of life, and certainly there are other issues too. Which issue or issues should we prioritize at the ballot box? Which is the right one to give less emphasis in a particular election year? Those are difficult questions that do not have clear answers. We must, in prudence, simply do our best while struggling in our consciences.

Yet in closing it is worth suggesting that there could be one preeminent issue that faces us. We must be careful about preeminent priorities for all the reasons that this book has named. It is ironic to name a preeminent priority now. Yet if there is one that the consistent ethic of life asks us to focus on, it is not abortion or any other issue. It is something else entirely.

A Better Kind of Politics

From the beginning of his papacy, Pope Francis has called on Catholics to think about social life in terms of solidarity.

He also has been encouraging us to embrace "a better kind of politics." These are related ideas, and they have a lot to do with the consistent ethic of life.

In *Evangelii Gaudium* (2013), Pope Francis linked our lives of faith to social and political life. "All Christians, their pastors included," he wrote, "are called to show concern for the building of a better world," and Pope Francis also went on to quote Pope Benedict XVI: "The just ordering of society and of the state is a central responsibility of politics," and the Church "cannot and must not remain on the sidelines in the fight for justice.[26] Pope Francis goes on in *Evangelii Gaudium* to say, "Politics, though often denigrated, remains a lofty vocation and one of the highest forms of charity."[27] He makes an impassioned appeal for just such a charitable politics and calls us all "to care for the vulnerable of the earth" because, as we learn in the parable of the Good Samaritan, the vulnerable make the most urgent and articulate claim on our concern, always. Yet perhaps even more important for us here, Pope Francis notes that "no government can act without regard for shared responsibility."[28]

It is the nature of politics and government that Francis continues to write about throughout his ministry. In *Laudato Si'* Francis reminded us of the "proper and inalienable responsibility" (38) of government to preserve the environment that belongs to everyone. Once again, Francis tells us "a healthy politics is needed" (181), and tells us that means "a politics which is farsighted and capable of a new, integral and interdisciplinary approach" (197). All of this needs to be understood together with *Fratelli Tutti*, where Pope Francis wrote about solidarity and "A Better Kind of Politics." The persistence of this theme should tell us something. Francis wants us to understand government and politics in a particular way, and understanding that is urgently important for Christian life in our time.

Pope Francis asks Catholics to have respect for politics. More than that, Francis wants Catholics to see and understand politics as a responsibility for everyone because it is politics that permits us to build up the world and pursue the common good. To protect human flourishing and human life, it takes a political community. No one defends the vulnerable alone: it takes organized, social action. Thus, to defend human life with an ethic of consistency presumes a healthy politics oriented toward the common good. Without a healthy politics oriented toward the common good, it simply is not possible to defend the lives and dignity of the vulnerable. Underneath all the questions that this book has addressed we find one necessary condition that must exist before we can be faithful citizens: that there is a political system operating according to the rule of law and that is responsive to the preferences of citizens who engage one another in political debate to make public policy through fair elections. Every issue that the consistent ethic of life might take up and ask us to consider depends on the idea that our consideration of those issues in the light of the consistent ethic can matter because there is a political system open to the participation of our well-formed consciences. Yet we know that our political system faces dangers today that we never would have imagined as recently as when the consistent ethic of life was first formulated. This should incite some concern among Catholics who take the consistent ethic of life seriously.

Politics itself is a preeminent priority. Politics and the political process is something we must defend. The reason we must defend politics is because, without it, we cannot hope to achieve justice or peace. Politics is how justice and peace are built in the world. Catholics cannot pursue our conscientious prudential judgments considering the consistent ethic without a political system that is open to participation. When Catholics mark a ballot, respect for life obliges them to choose candidates who respect what politics and government are, who will look beyond mere partisan advantage or narrow interest, and who are committed to using the opportunities politics and government present for the common good. Whether we mean election denials, voter suppression, or the widespread falsehoods that pollute our public discourse, our instinctive partisanship that finds us acting more like opponents than fellow citizens has placed politics itself in a new sort of danger today. Without a healthy politics, there can be no effective witness to human life.

The Catholic tradition has defended politics and government since long before Pope Francis, of course. Pope Francis in this way only builds on the constant understanding of the Catholic tradition that politics and government are intimately connected to human goods.[29] While the Catholic Church does not tell us that any one form of government the best form, recent teachings have emphasized how "praise is due to those national procedures which allow the largest possible number of citizens to participate in public affairs with genuine freedom," and sees "democracy as the most appropriate form of political order" when it results in law and policy that is "the expression of the common interest of all."[30] Of course there are complexities, and not every democratic decision is a morally good decision. Still, the Catholic Church increasingly recognizes the correspondence between the moral teaching that all human beings enjoy equal dignity before their Creator and the political implications of that teaching—that "government of the people, by the people, for the people" is the most morally acceptable form of government.

If we accept those propositions—

- that the defense of human life and the cultivation of human goods depends on a healthy politics

- that the Catholic Church always has taught us that government is good because it is the way we collaborate together toward the common good
- that a system of government inviting wide political participation with laws and rules protecting the rights of everyone is the most morally legitimate form of government because it recognizes the human dignity of every citizen

—then anything in political life that frustrates a healthy politics is opposed to the dignity of human life. Our politics must embrace wide participation, firm rules that protect the vulnerable so that their voices can be heard, and respect for the political process and its outcomes. Anything less than that is unacceptable, and the challenges our political system has faced in recent years suggest that our politics have become unacceptable, perhaps even morally wrong. It is not for nothing that Pope Francis has called Catholics to "a better kind of politics": the need is real. More than any particular issue facing Catholic citizens, in this way the health of our politics itself is the preeminent priority because no other good can be achieved without a better kind of politics than the one we have today.

Whether that preeminent priority persuades every reader or not, of course, is not the purpose of this book. Rather, this book's purpose is to do something that resembles what we find in a healthy politics. This book exists to propose an idea. The idea is not an idea about any political or social issue. Rather, the idea is about a way of seeing all social and political issues. It is about an understanding of who we are as individual persons and as a human community—members of a society and a creation whose indivisible source insists on our oneness and solidarity. This book is offered with the hope that it will encourage an attitude that all human life everywhere and in every circumstance is equally valuable to God, and that we must seek always to do the best we can do with our frail human capacities to defend life, promote the flourishing of life: In all that we do, to be an effective and consistent witness to life.

Conclusion

Some of this book's beginning can be found in a parish talk about the consistent ethic of life that I was invited to offer in July 2022. The date is worth mentioning because that talk profited by coincidence. The Mass readings for the previous Sunday were particularly appropriate for a conversation about the consistent ethic.[1]

The first reading was from Deuteronomy, and the reading took us to the end of the Israelites' forty years of wandering through the desert, when Moses just has finished giving them the law. The law is called the Deuteronomic Code because it comes from the Book of Deuteronomy, and it contains all sorts of detailed instructions about how God's people, the people of Israel, are meant to maintain their relationship with God. The Deuteronomic Code tells the Jewish people how to offer sacrifices, it gives rules about leprosy and about those who are ritually unclean, rules about diet, and other moral instructions about the duty to seek always after justice. But the selection we heard that Sunday came after all that. Our reading found Moses offering one final thought about the law. He said, "This commandment that I am commanding you today is not too hard for you….No, the word is very near to you; it is in your mouth and in your heart to observe" (Deut 30:11, 14).

A CONSISTENT ETHIC OF LIFE

The Deuteronomic Code Moses had just given to Israel is filled with complex details, and those details are important. But there is something more important than any of those complex details, and it is something simple. If we love God, and if we honor our relationship to God, then we already have achieved the most important thing because before we can keep the law in all its complexity and detail, we first must *want* to keep the law. And, if we *want* to keep the law then it is already in our mouths and in our hearts, and we only must carry it out. The law is an expression of our relationship to God, and, more important, keeping the law is an expression of our desire to be in relationship with God and honor that relationship. That really is what God wants. It is not very different from the consistent ethic of life.

The Gospel that Sunday offered us the parable of the Good Samaritan, just as we find it in Pope Francis's *Fratelli Tutti*. In that Gospel, a scholar of the law has asked Jesus what must be done to gain eternal life and Jesus answers in the words of the Jewish *shema*, an ancient prayer that is part of the daily prayer of observant Jews anywhere: "*You shall love the Lord your God with all your heart, with all your soul, with all your strength, and with all your mind; and your neighbor as yourself*" (Luke 10:27). The prayer amounts to the same simple affirmation we got from Moses in the first reading—keep your relationship with God—and, it adds an additional detail that we also find in the law: love "your neighbor as yourself."

Loving our neighbor this way is so closely related to keeping our relationship with God that it is in the same sentence: love God, love your neighbor. These are effectively the same thing because we don't encounter God face-to-face every day here in the world except for the way we encounter God every day in one another—the people God has created in God's image. And so, we honor our relationship to God by honoring our relationships with one another. The message of the parable tells us that. The priest and the Levite who walk past the beaten man have an obvious relationship to him: all three are Jews. The Samaritan has no obvious relationship to the beaten man, but he is the one who stops and cares for him. Jesus tells the story this way because the Samaritan reminds us of what we too often forget too easily: we all have a relationship with one another, whether we see it or not, because we all are created by the same God who loves each person God created in just the same way. When we honor our relationship with one another in this way, we honor our relationship to God.

The scholar of the law asked Jesus in the Gospel, "Who is my neighbor?" and Jesus's answer is simple: my neighbor is anyone I meet along the road whom God has put there with me. And, we may go further to say that our response to the people we meet along the road who need our care is not meant to be comfortable for us. The Samaritan caused himself no small discomfort when he responded to the beaten man God put before him. We do not choose the circumstances in which we are asked to honor our relationship to God by caring for one another. If we did, we would choose things that didn't inconvenience us at all. God wants something else from us. God wants us to show what is already in our mouths and in our hearts, and whether we will carry it out. We are asked constantly, Do we want to honor our relationship with God, not the way we like but the way God asks? Are we willing to do uncomfortable things that show what is in our mouth and in our heart when we carry them out?

This is the heart of the consistent ethic of life. Do we accept the challenges that God sets before us, to respond in solidarity as witnesses to life who *want* to be in relationship with God and with our neighbors? Can we be so converted to our faith that we abandon our partisan instincts to prefer all of the vulnerable always, in every situation? If our answer is yes, then our task at once becomes more complicated than any voters' guide and more simple. We respond. We simply respond, with prudence and consistency, we respond with love for the vulnerable. We study the problem, we pray and reflect, and then we choose the best way to use our vote or energy to do the most good we can do. It is not our actions themselves so much as our converted attitude that the consistent ethic emphasizes. And when we emphasize and act on that attitude, our behavior is different.

Part of what we are describing here is how necessary it is to let go of our partisan habits—thinking of issues in terms of Democratic or Republican or progressive or conservative positions. We must loosen our grip and abandon that habit of mind entirely! When we look at the long history of the consistent ethic we can quickly see why: so much of the rejection of the consistent ethic has come because the consistent ethic frustrates those partisan categories, and we find it hard to let go of them.

We can instead, respond to Pope Francis's call to prefer "fruitfulness" over "great results"—to be satisfied even if "I can help at least one person." If we can allow that to become our measure of success, allow our political engagement to be only one part of our greater spiritual life, then we are beginning to engage politics in a better way. When we do that, we always bear witness to life.

Notes

Preface

1. Joseph Cardinal Bernardin to Rev. Norman Bevan, CSSp (October 8, 1996), archives of Catholic Theological Union, Chicago.

2. Thomas A. Nairn, OFM, "Introduction," in *The Consistent Ethic of Life: Assessing Its Relevance and Reception*, ed. Thomas A. Nairn (Maryknoll, NY: Orbis Books, 2008), xiii.

Chapter One

1. See Marvin L. Krier Mich, *Catholic Social Teaching and Movements* (Mystic, CT: Twenty-Third Publications, 1998), 211–12. I am indebted to M. Therese Lysaught for pointing me to Egan's use of the seamless garment metaphor. See M. Therese Lysaught, "From *The Challenge of Peace* to *The Gift of Peace*: Reading the Consistent Ethic of Life as an Ethic of Peacemaking," in *The Consistent Ethic of Life: Assessing Its Reception and Relevance*, ed. Thomas A. Nairn (Maryknoll, NY: Orbis Books, 2008), 112–13.

2. Archbishop Humberto Medeiros, "A Call to a Consistent Ethic of Life and the Law," *Boston Pilot*, July 10, 1971, 7.

3. Edward B. Fiske, "War and the Clergy," *New York Times*, February 15, 1966, 2.

4. John T. Cogley, "Spellman Opposes Council Draft on Conscientious Objectors," *New York Times*, September 22, 1965, 17. See also Marjorie Hyer, "How Our War-Blessing Bishops Got Religion on Nukes," *Washington Post*, May 1, 1983, https://www.washingtonpost.com/archive/opinions/1983/05/01/how-our-war-blessing-catholic-bishops-got-religion-on-nukes/a9ec5e76-d679-4a9f-9806-f220b20c9b5e/.

5. Paul J. Hallinan and Joseph L. Bernardin, "War and Peace: A Pastoral Letter to the Archdiocese of Atlanta, October 1966," in *Documents of American Catholic History*, vol. 2, *1866–1966*, ed. John Tracy Ellis (Wilmington, DE: Michael Glazier, 1987), 696–702.

6. B. Drummond Ayres Jr., "Editor of The Catholic Reporter Dismissed in Dispute on Policy," *New York Times*, May 8, 1971, 18.

7. See Steven P. Millies, *Good Intentions: A History of Catholic Voters' Road from Roe to Trump* (Collegeville, MN: Liturgical Press, 2018), 22–23, 225–228n69.

8. Daniel K. Williams, *Defenders of the Unborn: The Pro-Life Movement before* Roe v. Wade (New York: Oxford University Press, 2016), 4.

9. Testimony of Cardinal John Cody, Committee on Constitutional Amendments of the Senate Committee on the Judiciary, *Abortion—Part I: Hearings on S.J. Res. 119 and S.J. Res. 130*, 93rd Cong., 2d sess., 1974, 226.

10. Archbishop Joseph Bernardin, "Homily for the Mass Commemorating the Feast of St. Francis de Sales, Patron of the Archdiocese," St. Peter in Chains Cathedral, Cincinnati, January 28, 1973, in the Archdiocese of Chicago Joseph Cardinal Bernardin Archive and Records Center, Chicago, Joseph Cardinal Bernardin Speeches and Talks Collection.

11. Archbishop Joseph Bernardin, "Homily for Mass Observing Second Anniversary of the Supreme Court's Abortion Decision," St. Peter in Chains Cathedral, Cincinnati, January 22, 1975, in Archdiocese of Chicago Joseph Cardinal Bernardin Archive and Records Center, Chicago, Joseph Cardinal Bernardin Speeches and Talks Collection.

12. Bernardin, "Homily for Mass Commemorating Third Anniversary of the Supreme Court's Abortion Decision," St. Peter in Chains Cathedral, Cincinnati, January 22, 1976, in Archdiocese of Chicago Joseph Cardinal Bernardin Archive and Records Center, Chicago, Joseph Cardinal Bernardin Speeches and Talks Collection.

13. John F. Kennedy to Ngo Dinh Diem, December 14, 1961, in Department of State Bulletin, January 1, 1962, 13–14.

14. Augustine, *Ep. ad Bonif.*, clxxxix.

15. J. Bryan Hehir, "Just War Theory in a Post-Cold War World," *Journal of Religious Ethics* 20, no. 2 (Fall 1992): 241.

16. Carlos M. N. Eire, *Reformations: The Early Modern World, 1450–1650* (New Haven, CT: Yale University Press, 2016), 378. Eire's history of the Reformation is dauntingly comprehensive but an indispensable resource.

17. For a particularly good, recent treatment, see Barry Hudock, *Struggle, Condemnation, Vindication: John Courtney Murray's Journey to Vatican II* (Collegeville, MN: Liturgical Press, 2015).

18. See John Courtney Murray, "Memo to Cushing on Contraception Legislation" in *Bridging the Sacred and the Secular*, ed. J. Leon Hooper, SJ (Washington, DC: Georgetown University Press, 1994), 237–47.

19. Cardinal Joseph Ratzinger made a similar point four decades later when he wrote that there is a "polyphonic relatedness" between different cultures that exhibit receptiveness to "the essential complementarity of reason and faith," and, "Ultimately, the essential values and norms that are in some

way known or sensed by all…will take on a new brightness," in *Dialectics of Secularization: On Reason and Religion*, by Jürgen Habermas and Joseph Ratzinger, ed. and trans. Florian Schuller (San Francisco: Ignatius Press, 2007), 79–80.

20. See John Courtney Murray, "The Issue of Church and State at Vatican Council II," *Theological Studies* 27 (December 1966): 580.

Chapter Two

1. For a full biography see Steven P. Millies, *Joseph Bernardin: Seeking Common Ground* (Collegeville, MN: Liturgical Press, 2016).

2. Joseph Cardinal Bernardin, *The Gift of Peace* (Chicago: Loyola Press, 1997).

3. J. Bryan Hehir, "From the Pastoral Constitution of Vatican II to *The Challenge of Peace*," in *Catholics and Nuclear War: A Commentary on The Challenge of Peace, the U.S. Bishops' Pastoral Letter on War and Peace*, ed. Philip J. Murnion (Crossroad: New York, 1983), 75.

4. See "Excerpts from Comments by Catholic Bishops on Issues of War and Peace," *New York Times*, November 19, 1982. Quoted were Bishop Alfred C. Hughes, Bishop Richard J. Sklba, Bishop Michael Kenny, Bishop Joseph A. Fiorenza, Bishop James W. Malone, Bishop Roger Mahony, Archbishop Edward A. McCarthy, Archbishop Oscar H. Lipscomb, Archbishop James A. Hickey, and Bishop Joseph M. Sullivan.

5. Hehir, "From the Pastoral Constitution of Vatican II to *The Challenge of Peace*," 75.

6. In part, we could say that this was a result of growing divisions among bishops that mirrored the growing divisions among Catholics in the United States. For at least a partial description see Steven P. Millies, *Good Intentions: A History of Catholic Voters' Road from Roe to Trump* (Collegeville, MN:

Liturgical Press, 2018), 62–65. But we also should note this ability was lost in a formal sense by 1998, when Pope John Paul II all but foreclosed the possibility of a bishops' conference acting together in this way in a *motu proprio* titled *Apostolos Suos*.

7. Mary McGrory, "WAR," *Washington Post*, November 18, 1982.

8. Kenneth A. Briggs, "Bishop Support Plan by Hatch to Curb Abortions," *New York Times*, November 19, 1981.

9. National Conference of Catholic Bishops/U.S. Catholic Conference, Pastoral Letter *The Challenge of Peace: God's Promise and Our Response*, Summary.

10. Briggs, "Bishop Support Plan by Hatch."

11. Briggs, "Bishop Support Plan by Hatch."

12. For a full description of Bernardin, the bishops, and how the 1976 presidential campaign launched the abortion politics of ensuing decades, see Millies, *Good Intentions*, 47–53.

13. Memorandum from J. Bryan Hehir to the Most Reverend Joseph L. Bernardin, September 5, 1976, American Catholic History Research Center, NCCB Collection, Box 63, Folder "Ad Hoc Committee on Pro-Life Activities, Jul.–Sept. 1976," 2.

14. Another way to say this would be to say that the consistent ethic of life is a very visible and bold approach to what is called public theology, the presentation of what believers believe in the public square, outside the Church, much as St. Paul presented the gospel to the philosophers of Athens in Acts 17:16–34.

15. Joseph Cardinal Bernardin, "Catholic Teaching on World Order: Keeping and Building the Peace," article in the *festschrift* in honor of His Eminence, Agostino Cardinal Casaroli (undated typescript) at Joseph Cardinal Bernardin Archives and Records Center, Archdiocese of Chicago, Executive Records—CBC Administrative Files—Talks and Articles: Misc. Authors,

Box 45385.03, Folder 28 "Catholic Teaching on World Order: Keeping and Building the Peace: Article" in *Pro Fide et Justitia: Festschrift für Agostino Kardinal Casaroli zum 70. Geburtstag*, ed. Herbert Schambeck (Berlin: Dunker & Humblot, 1984), 3.

16. Cardinal Joseph L. Bernardin, "A Consistent Ethic of Life: An American Catholic Dialogue," Gannon Lecture, Fordham University, December 6, 1983, in *The Seamless Garment: Writings on the Consistent Ethic of Life*, ed. Thomas A. Nairn (Maryknoll, NY: Orbis Books, 2008), 7.

17. Bernardin, "A Consistent Ethic of Life," 8.

18. Bernardin, "A Consistent Ethic of Life," 10.

19. Bernardin, "A Consistent Ethic of Life," 11.

20. Origen, *Contra Celsum*, VIII:73.

21. In general, we could say that Augustine adapted Christianity to the needs of being in and governing the world. His treatment of lying is an important case for understanding this because it parallels his treatment of war and violence so closely. Deceit is discouraged as much as violence by Scripture, but Augustine found that one could lie for good reasons, such as to preserve life. In all, Augustine's realism concerned itself with describing a Christianity that could live in the world by making some moral compromises in pursuit of higher moral aims. Lying and killing always remain evil acts, but we may do them when circumstances require them so that greater goods may be obtained. See Augustine, *De Mendacio*.

22. Augustine, *De Civ.Dei*, XIX:12.

23. See Aquinas, *Summa Theologiae* II–II, q.40. Generally, the conditions for a just war divide into two categories: *jus ad bellum* (just reasons for war) and *jus in bello* (conducting war justly). To have a just reason for war, the war must be sought by a proper authority, there must be a just cause (such as self-defense), there must be a reasonable prospect for success, and war must be the last resort. In general, to conduct

just war refers to using proportionate levels of force that are adapted only to securing a victory and minimizing suffering. This also includes the avoidance of noncombatants and the humane treatment of prisoners.

24. In the revised edition of *Political Liberalism*, Rawls acknowledged that the consistent ethic satisfied the conditions of public reason because it "includes these three political values: public peace, essential protections of human rights, and the commonly accepted standards of behaviors in a community of law." See John Rawls, *Political Liberalism*, rev. ed. (New York: Columbia University Press, 2005), 480.

25. Marjorie Hyer, "Bernardin Views Prolife Issues as 'Seamless Garment,'" *Washington Post*, December 10, 1983.

26. Hyer, "Bernardin Views Prolife Issues as 'Seamless Garment.'"

27. Hyer, "Bernardin Views Prolife Issues as 'Seamless Garment.'"

28. Mario Cuomo, "Religious Belief and Public Morality: A Catholic Governor's Perspective," John A. O'Brien Lecture, Department of Theology, University of Notre Dame, September 13, 1984. Published in Richard W. Conklin, *A Report on Religion from the University of Notre Dame Department of Public Relations and Information* IV:1 (Fall 1984).

29. Cuomo, "Religious Belief and Public Morality."

30. The Week, *National Review* (December 13, 1985), 10.

31. James Hitchcock, "Abortion and the Catholic Church," *Human Life Review* 12, no. 7 (Winter 1986): 64.

32. Joseph Sobran, "The 'Seamless Garment' Revisited," *Sobran's Real News of the Month*, August 16, 2005, http://www.sobran.com/columns/2005/050816.shtml.

33. Richard John Neuhaus, "John Cardinal O'Connor, 1920–2000," *First Things*, https://www.firstthings.com/web-exclusives/2008/05/john-cardinal-oconnor.

34. John Hirschauer, "Bill Barr Tears the Seamless Garment," *National Review*, June 22, 2020, https://www.nationalreview .com/2020/06/bill-barr-death-penalty-catholic-critics-attack -attorney-generals-faith/.

35. Kenneth A. Briggs, "Bernardin Asks Catholics to Fight Both Nuclear Arms and Abortion," *New York Times*, December 7, 1983.

Chapter Three

1. That compilation is Cardinal Joseph L. Bernardin, *The Seamless Garment: Writings on the Consistent Ethic of Life*, ed. Thomas A. Nairn (Maryknoll, NY: Orbis Books, 2008).

2. Thomas A. Nairn, "Introduction," *The Consistent Ethic of Life: Assessing Its Reception and Relevance*, ed. Thomas A. Nairn (Maryknoll, NY: Orbis Books, 2008), xii.

3. Cardinal Joseph L. Bernardin, "A Consistent Ethic of Life: Continuing the Dialogue" in *Seamless Garment*, 19.

4. Bernardin, "A Consistent Ethic of Life: Continuing the Dialogue," in *Seamless Garment*, 17.

5. See *Origins*, November 8, 1984, 326.

6. Cardinal Joseph L. Bernardin, "Linkage and the Logic of the Abortion Debate," Address for the Right-to-Life Conference, Kansas City, MO, June 7, 1984, in *Seamless Garment*, 23, 24, 25.

7. Cardinal Joseph L Bernardin, "The Consistent Ethic of Life and Public Policy," Address for the U.S. Catholic Conference Social Action Director's Conference, Washington, DC, February 10, 1988, in *Seamless Garment*, 147.

8. Bernardin, "Consistent Ethic of Life and Public Policy," in *Seamless Garment*, 147–49, passim.

9. Bernardin, "Reflections on the Public Life and Witness of the Church in U.S. Society and Culture," Address at

Georgetown University, Washington, DC, September 9, 1996, in *Seamless Garment*, 288, 287.

10. Bernardin, "Reflections on the Public Life and Witness of the Church," in *Seamless Garment*, 297, 294–95.

11. Bernardin, "The Church's Witness to Life," Address at Seattle University, Seattle, March 2, 1986, in *Seamless Garment*, 107.

12. Early references to the consistent ethic of life can be found among several writers in the academic literature immediately after Bernardin's Gannon Lecture, though the earliest of them do not engage in any substantive reflection we should note here. Those include Zoë Sofia, "Exterminating Fetuses: Abortion, Disarmament, and the Sexo-Semiotics of Extraterrestrialism," *Diacritics* 14, no. 2 (Summer 1984): 47–59; Christine E. Gudorf, "To Make a Seamless Garment, Use a Single Piece of Cloth," *CrossCurrents* 34, no. 4 (Winter 1984–85): 473–91; John F. Kane, "Some Reflections on the American Catholic Bishops' Peace Pastoral," *Dialogue: A Journal of Mormon Theology* (Winter 1984): 37–45; and Susan Dowell, "II—Prolifers for Survival," *New Blackfriars* 66, no. 776 (February 1985): 67–72.

13. Mary F. Segers, "The Catholic Bishops' Pastoral Letter on War and Peace: A Feminist Perspective," *Feminist Studies* 11, no. 3 (Autumn 1985): 635–36.

14. Brenda D. Hofman, "Political Theology: The Role of Organized Religion in the Anti-abortion Movement," *Journal of Church and State* 28, no. 2 (Spring 1986): 229.

15. William V. D'Antonio, "The American Catholic Family: Signs of Cohesion and Polarization," *Journal of Marriage and Family* 47, no. 2 (May 1985): 400.

16. Heinz R. Kuehn, "Catholic Itinerary," *The American Scholar* 55, no. 4 (Autumn 1986): 486, 489–90.

17. Kuehn, "Catholic Itinerary," 490.

18. Kuehn, "Catholic Itinerary," 486, and D'Antonio, "American Catholic Family," 401.

19. Dan Hortsch, "Catholics at UP Conference Told Dignity Should Be Guide on Issues," *The Oregonian*, October 5, 1986.

20. Hortsch, "Catholics at UP Conference."

21. Hortsch, "Catholics at UP Conference."

22. Hortsch, "Catholics at UP Conference."

23. "We have no direct information about the event," and, "We have no program or publicity for the event. The student newspaper did not notice or report on the conference," in Rev. Jeffrey Schneibel, CSC, University of Portland archivist, email message to author, January 24, 2023. Similarly, the archivist for the archdiocese of Cincinnati was able to provide only a few extant materials among the papers of Archbishop Daniel Pilarczyk.

24. "Conference Sponsors Life Ethic Program," *Cincinnati Catholic Telegraph*, May 20, 1988.

25. "Conference Sponsors Life Ethic Program."

26. John Finnis, "The Consistent Ethic—a Philosophical Critique" in *Consistent Ethic of Life*, ed. Thomas G. Fuechtmann (Kansas City: Sheed & Ward, 1988), 146.

27. Finnis, "Consistent Ethic," 141–42, passim.

28. Finnis, "Consistent Ethic," 166, 163.

29. Address of Patrick J. Buchanan to the Republican National Convention, Houston, August 17, 1992.

30. Barack Obama, *The Audacity of Hope: Thoughts on Reclaiming the American Dream* (New York: Crown, 2006), 36.

31. Sen. Edward M. Kennedy, *Congressional Record*, S. 18519 (July 1, 1987).

32. Buchanan, Address to the Republican National Convention.

33. Maureen Dowd, "G.O.P.'s Rising Star in the House Pledges to Right the Wrongs of the Left," *New York Times,* November 10, 1994.

34. "Understanding the Difference," *First Things* 198, December 1, 2009, 68.

35. Peter Steinfels, "Catholic Bishops' Taxing Task: Election-Year Statement," *New York Times,* October 27, 2007.

36. Steinfels, "Catholic Bishops' Taxing Task."

37. See Darrin W Snyder Belousek, "Toward a Consistent Ethic of Life in the Peace Tradition Perspective: A Critical-Constructive Response to the MC USA Statement on Abortion," *Mennonite Quarterly Review* 79, no. 4 (2005): 439–80.

38. Regina Wentzel Wolfe, "Ministering in a Divided Church: Can the Consistent Ethic of Life Bridge the Contention?," in Nairn, *Consistent Ethic,* 98.

39. Wolfe, "Ministering in a Divided Church," 106.

40. James J. Walter, "What Does Horizon Analysis Bring to the Consistent Ethic of Life?," in Nairn, *Consistent Ethic,* 15.

41. Walter, "What Does Horizon Analysis Bring?," 11.

42. Walter, "What Does Horizon Analysis Bring?," 11.

43. Thomas A. Nairn, OFM, "The Consistent Ethic of Life as Moral Analogy," in Nairn, *Consistent Ethic,* 37, 39, 36.

44. "It may very well be that Bernardin saw a danger in his use of analogy, that it would take him where he did not want to go—or to where he felt that, as a spokesperson for the Catholic Church, could not go." Nairn, "Consistent Ethic of Life as Moral Analogy," 47.

45. M. Therese Lysaught, "From *The Challenge of Peace* to *The Gift of Peace*: Reading the Consistent Ethic of Life as an Ethic of Peacemaking" in Nairn, *Consistent Ethic,* 128.

Chapter Four

1. See U.S. Conference of Catholic Bishops, "Theology of the Body Overview," https://www.usccb.org/issues-and-action/marriage-and-family/natural-family-planning/catholic-teaching/theology-of-the-body.

2. Cardinal Christoph Schönborn, OP, "Pope's New Book, Jesus of Nazareth, Published in English," *L'Osservatore Romano*, English edition, May 30, 2007.

3. George Weigel, *Witness to Hope: The Biography of Pope John Paul II, 1920–2005* (New York: Perennial, 2005), 756.

4. Cardinal Joseph Ratzinger, "'The Problem of Threats to Human Life,'" Address to the Extraordinary Consistory of Cardinals, *L'Osservatore Romano*, April 8, 1991.

5. Fox Butterfield, "Massachusetts Is Asked to Ease Abortion Laws," *New York Times*, September 21, 1991. Also, Message of the Holy Father Pope John Paul II for the VIII World Youth Day, August 15, 1993, 5.

6. Quoted in Weigel, *Witness to Hope*, 757.

7. *Catechism of the Catholic Church* (New York: Catholic Book Publishing Company, 1994), 2267.

8. Weigel, *Witness to Hope*, 758.

9. *Evangelium Vitae* 56, quoting *Catechism* 2266.

10. *Evangelium Vitae* 56, quoting *Catechism* 2267. Here we should note that *Evangelium Vitae* did allow for the death penalty "in cases of absolute 'necessity'" (56). Sister Helen Prejean, CSJ seized on this language in a January 1, 1997, letter to Pope John Paul II, writing that "Justice Antonin Scalia, who is relentless in his pursuit of legalizing executions, even of juveniles and the mentally retarded, and who expedites the death process in the courts in every way he can…seems to have no trouble squaring executions with his Catholic faith," and, going on, she adds, "When in *Evangelium Vitae*, paragraph 56, you uphold the state's right to execute in cases of

'absolute necessity,' some pro-death penalty advocates such as Catholic District Attorney of New Orleans, Harry Connick, Sr. use those words to justify their vigorous pursuit of the death penalty." Sister Helen Prejean, CSJ, to Pope John Paul II, January 1, 1997, Sr. Helen Prejean Papers, Box 1, Folder 3, DePaul University Special Collections and Archives Department, Chicago. Sister Helen's efforts paid off. During an apostolic journey to the United States in 1999, Pope John Paul II preached a homily in which he said, "The new evangelization calls for followers of Christ who are unconditionally pro-life: who will proclaim, celebrate and serve the Gospel of life in every situation. A sign of hope is the increasing recognition that the dignity of human life must never be taken away, even in the case of someone who has done great evil. Modern society has the means of protecting itself, without definitively denying criminals the chance to reform (cf. *Evangelium Vitae* 27). I renew the appeal I made most recently at Christmas for a consensus to end the death penalty, which is both cruel and unnecessary," Homily, January 27, 1999, 5, https://www.vatican.va/content/john-paul-ii/en/homilies/1999/documents/hf_jp-ii_hom_19990127_stlouis.html. Of course, that homily does not reflect an official, magisterial teaching. The importance of the homily and noting these details and developments here is to underscore that John Paul was thinking about the death penalty this way while *Evangelium Vitae* was being drafted and received.

11. *Evangelium Vitae* 87.

12. Rev. Michael D. Place, interview by Steven P. Millies, December 12, 2022, Chicago. Also Rev. Michael D. Place, email to author, April 30, 2023. Bernardin had traveled with a delegation from Chicago on pilgrimage to Jerusalem March 20–27, 1995.

13. See Catholic Bishops of Aotearoa New Zealand, Pastoral Statement, "*Te Kahu o te Ora*: A Consistent Ethic of Life"

(2023). See also Catholic Bishops of Aotearoa New Zealand, Pastoral Statement, *Te Kahu o te Ora*: A Consistent Ethic of Life" (1997). Note that the titles of both statements are the same.

14. United States Conference of Catholic Bishops, "Forming Consciences for Faithful Citizenship: A Call to Political Responsibility from the Catholic Bishops of the United States" (Washington, DC: United States Conference of Catholic Bishops, 2019), 6, 8, 15, 24. Also, Anthony R. Picarello Jr., USCCB Associate General Secretary & General Counsel, to author, December 28, 2016, 2.

15. George Weigel, "The End of the Bernardin Era: The Rise, Dominance, and Decline of a Culturally Accommodating Catholicism," *First Things*, February 2011, https://www.firstthings.com/article/2011/02/the-end-of-the-bernardin-era.

16. Archbishop Gerhard Muller quoted in Mark Shea, "The Seamless Garment: What It Is and What It Isn't," *National Catholic Register*, July 14, 2014, https://www.ncregister.com/blog/the-seamless-garment-what-it-is-and-isn-t.

17. John Hirschauer, "Bill Barr Tears the Seamless Garment," *National Review*, June 22, 2020, https://www.nationalreview.com/2020/06/bill-barr-death-penalty-catholic-critics-attack-attorney-generals-faith/.

18. Cardinal Joseph L. Bernardin, "The Church's Witness to Life," Seattle University, March 2, 1986, in Joseph L. Bernardin, *The Seamless Garment: Writings on the Consistent Ethic of Life*, ed. Thomas A. Nairn (Maryknoll, NY: Orbis Books, 2008), 103.

19. Pope John Paul II, "Homily of His Holiness Pope John Paul II," Cherry Creek State Park, Denver, August 15, 1993, 4, https://www.vatican.va/content/john-paul-ii/en/homilies/1993/documents/hf_jp-ii_hom_19930815_gmg-denver.html.

20. The lecture was published subsequently in *Commonweal*. See Cardinal Blase Cupich, "Signs of the Times: Witnessing to a Consistent Ethic of Solidarity," *Commonweal*, June 2, 2017, 14.

21. See U.S. Conference of Catholic Bishops, "Seven Themes of Catholic Social Teaching," https://www.usccb .org/beliefs-and-teachings/what-we-believe/catholic-social -teaching/seven-themes-of-catholic-social-teaching.

22. See Aquinas, *Summa Theologiae* II–II, 58, 9. Also John 17:22–23.

23. See Steven P. Millies, "Friendship with God and One Another: The Consistent Ethic of Solidarity in Historical, Political, and Theological Perspective," *Chicago Studies* 58, no. 1 (Spring/Summer 2019): 32–43, especially 33–34.

24. *Compendium of the Social Doctrine of the Church*, 19.

25. Cupich, "Signs of the Times," 14, quoting John Paul II, *Sollicitudo Rei Socialis* 39. See elsewhere in *Sollicitudo*: "It is above all a question of interdependence, sensed as a system determining relationships in the contemporary world, in its economic, cultural, political and religious elements, and accepted as a moral category. When interdependence becomes recognized in this way, the correlative response as a moral and social attitude, as a 'virtue,' is solidarity. This then is not a feeling of vague compassion or shallow distress at the misfortunes of so many people, both near and far. On the contrary, it is a firm and persevering determination to commit oneself to the common good; that is to say to the good of all and of each individual, because we are all really responsible for all. This determination is based on the solid conviction that what is hindering full development is that desire for profit and that thirst for power already mentioned. These attitudes and 'structures of sin' are only conquered—presupposing the help of divine grace—by a diametrically opposed attitude: a commitment to the good of one's neighbor with the readiness, in the

gospel sense, to 'lose oneself' for the sake of the other instead of exploiting him, and to 'serve him' instead of oppressing him for one's own advantage (cf. Mt 10:40–42; 20:25; Mk 10:42–45; Lk 22:25–27)," 38.

26. Cardinal Blase J. Cupich, "The Bond of Perfection: From the Consistent Ethic of Life to an Integral Ethic of Solidarity," remarks at Fordham University, New York (September 27, 2023).

27. Cupich, "The Bond of Perfection."

28. Rev. Michael D. Place, interview by Steven P. Millies, December 12, 2022, Chicago.

29. Cupich, "Signs of the Times," 14.

30. *Sollicitudo Rei Socialis* 38.

31. Cupich, "Signs of the Times," 16.

32. *Laudato Si'* 138 (hereafter referred to in the text as *LS*).

33. I am in debt to Rev. James Martin, SJ, for this summation. See James Martin, SJ (@jamesmartinsj), 2020, "Here's my one-line summary: If the message of 'Laudato Si' was 'Everything is connected,' the message of 'Fratelli Tutti' is 'Everyone is connected'" (October 16, 2020, 08:36am) https://twitter.com/JamesMartinSJ/status/1317097136220217346.

34. *Fratelli Tutti* 18. Quoting Pope Francis, "Address to the Diplomatic Corps Accredited to the Holy See," January 11, 2016, 120.

35. *Fratelli Tutti* 25, 29. Quoting from *Document on Human Fraternity for World Peace and Living Together*, Abu Dhabi, February 4, 2019, *L'Osservatore Romano*, February 4–5, 2019.

36. *Fratelli Tutti* 116, 115. Quoting Pope Francis, "Address to Participants in the Meeting of Popular Movements," October 28, 201), and Pope Francis, "Homily," Havana, Cuba, September 20, 2015: *L'Osservatore Romano*, September 21–22, 2015.

37. We would want to note here that this parable, while an important expression of Christian teaching found in the gospel and known widely by Christians everywhere, also is a

story that Jewish hearers sometimes encounter as a critique of Jews and Jewish ritual. The too-common interpretation of the parable—that the priest and the Levite passed by the beaten man because of their inordinate preoccupation with purity under the law—is not justified by a Jewish understanding and has been one of several subtle sources of antisemitism in Christian Scripture. In fact, nothing in the Jewish law would have justified abandoning the vulnerable victim of a robbery. Jesus's point in telling the story was not that the Samaritan was good, while the priest and the Levite were "bad" because they were so preoccupied by Jewish tradition. Quite the reverse, Jesus was highlighting how the Jewish tradition is good and those characters had lost their own moral compass. I am enlightened about this by my friend and colleague Malka Zeiger Simkovich. The work of Amy-Jill Levine on this topic is worth consulting. See Amy-Jill Levine, *Short Stories by Jesus: The Enigmatic Parables of a Controversial Rabbi* (New York: HarperOne, 2014).

38. Cardinal Joseph L. Bernardin, "Linkage and the Logic of the Abortion Debate," Address for the Right-to-Life Conference, Kansas City, MO, June 7, 1984, in *The Seamless Garment*, 25.

39. See Editorial, "The Pope on Panhandling: Give without Worry," *New York Times*, March 3, 2017, https://www.nytimes.com/2017/03/03/opinion/the-pope-on-panhandling-give-without-worry.html.

40. *Fratelli Tutti* 180 (hereafter referred to in the text as *FT*).

Chapter Five

1. *Gaudium et Spes* 53.
2. *Christifidelis Laici* 44.
3. *Christifidelis Laici* 54.

4. Joseph Cardinal Ratzinger, "Doctrinal Note on Some Questions Regarding the Participation of Catholics in Public Life," Congregation for the Doctrine of the Faith, November 24, 2002, 4.

5. "What I am saying here is that the complicated social affairs of the present day do require the moral guidance of the clergy; this is their great role. The means used, however, must be adapted to the age and climate in which we live. Clerical threats and fulminations either fall on deaf ears or arouse violent resentments even when a genuine moral issue is involved," in Jerome G. Kerwin, *Politics, Government, Catholics* (New York: Paulist Press, 1961), 86. Kerwin was a political scientist and the first Roman Catholic appointed to the University of Chicago faculty. His thoughtful reflections on the Church-state question deserve renewed attention in these days after the *Dobbs v. Jackson* decision that reversed *Roe v. Wade*.

6. José Casanova, *Public Religions in the Modern World* (Chicago: The University of Chicago Press, 1994), 205.

7. *Amoris Laetitia* 37.

8. Casanova, *Public Religions in the Modern World*, 206.

9. Casanova, *Public Religions in the Modern World*, 207. The bishops' "lobbying was mainly carried out via the National Right to Life Committee, created in 1973 as an entity distinct from the Church—something of a legal fiction....The tide turned definitively in 1980, when the issue assumed an overtly partisan cast, with the Republican Party officially committed to overturning *Roe* and the Democrats committed to its protection. Allied with evangelicals, new recruits to the cause, Catholic antiabortion activists cast their fortunes with the Republican Party, even as it drifted right with regard to other social policies," Leslie Woodcock Tentler, *American Catholics: A History* (New Haven, CT: Yale University Press, 2020), 325–26. For a full account of the bishops' turn

to lobbying and political pressure, see Steven P. Millies, *Good Intentions: A History of Catholics' Road from Roe to Trump* (Collegeville, MN: Liturgical Press, 2018), 32–61.

10. Edward L. Cleary, "Religion at the Statehouse: The California Catholic Conference," *Journal of Church and State* 45, no. 1 (2003): 44.

11. Cleary, "Religion at the Statehouse," 41.

12. Form 990, Return of Organization Exempt from Income Tax (2020) filed by the Minnesota Catholic Conference, accessible online at https://apps.irs.gov/pub/epostcard/cor/611664211_202006_990O_2022032919808765.pdf.

13. Form 990, Return of Organization Exempt from Income Tax (2018) filed by the California Catholic Conference, accessible online at https://apps.irs.gov/pub/epostcard/cor/271530655_201812_990O_2019083016610483.pdf.

14. Ken Godwin, Scott Ainsworth, and Erik K. Godwin, *Lobbying and Policymaking: The Public Pursuit of Private Interests* (Washington, DC: CQ Press, 2012), 11. The authors are political scientists. One of them spent a portion of his career as a lobbyist.

15. See U.S. Conference of Catholic Bishops, "Political Responsibility: Reflections on an Election Year (1976)," https://www.usccb.org/offices/justice-peace-human-development/political-responsibility-reflections-election-year-1976.

16. Quoting Pope Paul VI, "A Call to Action" (1971), 24.

17. See U.S. Conference of Catholic Bishops, "Faithful Citizenship: Civic Responsibility for a New Millennium (1999)," https://www.usccb.org/offices/justice-peace-human-development/faithful-citizenship-civic-responsibility-new-millennium.

18. A thorough and lengthy account of the history of those sanctions during this period may be found in Patricia Miller,

Good Catholics: The Battle over Abortion in the Catholic Church (Berkeley: University of California Press, 2014), 155–58.

19. See Brian Knowlton, "Would This Iraq Conflict Be a 'Just War'? Debate Swirls in U.S.," *New York Times*, March 7, 2003. https://www.nytimes.com/2003/03/07/news/would-this -iraq-conflict-be-a-just-wardebate-swirls-in-us.html. Catholics supporting the invasion in those days included Joe Biden, John Boehner, John Breaux, Dick Durbin, Paul Ryan, and Rick Santorum. Exact numbers are impossible to determine, and estimates vary concerning civilian deaths that resulted from U.S. military action in Iraq between 2003 and 2011. One reputable source, conducted through the Watson Institute for International & Public Affairs at Brown University, found the number of civilian deaths to be between 280,771 and 315,190. Some substantial number of those deaths, of course, were children or pregnant women. There were other costs, too. In 2007, Oxfam found that the child malnutrition rate had reached 28 percent in Iraq, and a University of Baghdad study estimated that 60–70 percent of Iraqi children had suffered psychological injuries because of the elective and "unjust" invasion that many U.S. Catholics supported in 2003.

20. See "Introductory Letter," *Forming Consciences for Faithful Citizenship: A Call to Political Responsibility from the Catholic Bishops of the United States* (Washington, DC: United States Conference of Catholic Bishops, 2019), 6.

21. *Summa Theologiae* II–II, 47, 2.

22. *Catechism of the Catholic Church*, 1806.

23. Michael Lipka and Gregory A. Smith, "Like Americans Overall, U.S. Catholics Are Divided by Party," *Pew Research Center*, January 24, 2019, https://www.pewresearch .org/short-reads/2019/01/24/like-americans-overall-u-s -catholics-are-sharply-divided-by-party/.

24. Katie Yoder, "Catholic Bishops' Pro-Life Chair Supports 15-Week Abortion Ban Nationwide," *Catholic News*

Agency, September 30, 2022, https://www.catholicnewsagency .com/news/252436/catholic-bishops-pro-life-chair-supports -15-week-abortion-ban-nationwide. The Centers for Disease Control found that 95 percent of U.S. abortions in 2019 occurred before the fifteenth week. See Brittany Shammas, Aaron Steckelberg, and Daniela Santamariña, "The Most Common Abortion Procedures and When They Occur," *Washington Post*, June 24, 2022, https://www.washingtonpost .com/health/2022/06/21/abortion-procedures/.

25. Archbishop William E. Lori, quoted in U.S. Conference of Catholic Bishops, "U.S. Bishops' Pro-Life Chairman Affirms Church Teaching on Dignity of Human Life," October 4, 2022, https://www.usccb.org/news/2022/us-bishops-pro-life -chairman-affirms-Church-teaching-dignity-human-life.

26. *Evangelii Gaudium* 183. Quoting from *Deus Caritas Est* 28.

27. *Evangelii Gaudium* 205.

28. *Evangelii Gaudium* 206.

29. "To believers, this point is settled: considered in itself, this human activity [government and political life] accords with God's will," in Pontifical Council for Justice and Peace, *Compendium of the Social Doctrine of the Church*, 456. See also *Gaudium et Spes* 34; *Pacem in Terris* 51–52; Aquinas, *Summa Theol.* Ia–IIae, q. 93., a.3 ad 2um.

30. See *Gaudium et Spes* 31. Also Joseph Card. Ratzinger, "That Which Holds the World Together: The Pre-political Moral Foundations of a Free State," in Jürgen Habermas and Joseph Ratzinger, *The Dialectics of Secularization: On Reason and Religion* (San Francisco: Ignatius Press, 2006), 59.

Conclusion

1. The readings were for the Fifteenth Sunday in Ordinary time in Year C (Lectionary 105).